SCANDALOUS: *breaking with propriety*

Audacious *bold, determined, beyond reasonable limits*

Extravagant *crazy, out-of-bounds, profuse*

GRACE: *a virtue of God*

Preposterous *undeserved, outrageous, unexpected*

Life-changing *wild, liberating, unrestrained, satisfying*

To Erin,

May you know the lavish riches of His grace!

Julie Ann Barnhill

1/31/06

$\mathcal{J}$ulie's sassy, hilarious, shoot-from-the-hip style is the real deal as she writes about real life—no sugar-coating, no "church language," no list of "shoulds"—infused with God's grace.

$\mathcal{B}$ring on Julie Barnhill—in spades! Can we clone her? Anyone who reads *Scandalous Grace* will feel like Julie is a best friend for life! Fill up a bubble bath, light a candle, make some hot tea, and soak in this wonderful book about God's outrageous, scandalous love for his daughters.

$\mathcal{F}$or too long Christian authors have sat high on their spiritual pedestals. Julie Ann Barnhill is down here in the dressing rooms of life, gasping in horror with the rest of us. *Scandalous Grace* is a welcome relief to everyone who is tired of striving to be something "more". . .and that's pretty much all of us.

$\mathcal{J}$ulie is totally truthful and hilariously honest about the issues that often send women down a spiral of shame and guilt.

$\mathcal{D}$oes the Gospel have anything to say about stretch marks? According to Julie Barnhill, the answer is yes! (God also has a few words about the boyfriend blues and the dressing-room dumps.) As always, Julie is breezy, funny, and very wise. For a good-time girlfriend read, curl up with this book.

OTHER BOOKS
BY JULIE ANN BARNHILL

She's Gonna Blow! Real Help for Moms Dealing with Anger

'Til Debt Do Us Part

Scandalous grace

Celebrate the liberating and
tantalizing realities of divine grace!

JULIE ANN BARNHILL

TYNDALE HOUSE PUBLISHERS, INC.
WHEATON, ILLINOIS

Visit Tyndale's exciting Web site at www.tyndale.com

Published in association with the literary agency of Alive Communications, Inc., 7680 Goddard Street, Suite 200, Colorado Springs, CO 80920.

Edited by Ramona Cramer Tucker

Designed by Jenny Swanson

The excerpt appearing on pages 33–37 is taken from *What's So Amazing About Grace?* hardcover (pp. 49–51) by Philip D. Yancey. Copyright © 1997 by Philip D. Yancey. Used by permission of Zondervan.

Unless otherwise noted, Scripture quotations are taken from *THE MESSAGE.* Copyright © 1993, 1994, 1995, 1996, 2000, 2001, 2002. Used by permission of NavPress Publishing Group.

Scripture quotations marked NASB are taken from the *New American Standard Bible,* © 1960, 1962, 1963, 1968, 1971, 1972, 1973, 1975, 1977 by The Lockman Foundation. Used by permission. All rights reserved.

Library of Congress Cataloging-in-Publication Data

Barnhill, Julie Ann, date.
  Scandalous grace / Julie Ann Barnhill.
    p. cm.
Includes bibliographical references.
ISBN 0-8423-8297-6 (pbk.)
1. Christian women—Religious life. 2. Grace (Theology) I. Title.
BV4527 .B365 2004
248.8′43—dc21   2003011974

Printed in the United States of America

09 08 07 06 05 04
7   6   5   4   3   2   1

To Audrey,
who has kept my darkest secrets—
sojourned through the scorched places—
and embodied the glorious reality
of scandalous grace.

CONTENTS

ᏋCKNOWLEDGMENTS

Ꮛt all began when I was a small child. . . ."

I don't so much write books as I first live them. The road to *Scandalous Grace* has been a long time in the living, and there are countless men and women who have walked with me along the way.

Thanks to *Grandma Bonnie,* who first demonstrated the lavishness and grace of unconditional love.

Rick, Kristen, Ricky Neal, and *Patrick,* who once again endured a wife and mother who forgot to do laundry, but extended enormous amounts of grace and continued both to love and speak to me.

Joan Johnson, who always made me feel like one of her girls.

Cindy Johnson Collier, who has watched me walk this road of faith—and stayed with me in the process.

Lesa Ward Cruzado and *Lisa Clark,* who believed my big mouth could actually work to my advantage someday down the road.

My Bible-study girlfriends, *Valerie Cooper, Anne Hess, Beth Ferguson, Cynthia Rauschert, Colleen and Velynna Spangler*—you listened to chapter ideas, dared to share your secrets, and maintained all of mine. I love you dearly.

Steve and *Carol Cramer*—unfettered access to their lakeside retreat helped me develop the initial proposal for *Scandalous Grace* as well as a summer tan.

The Adult Women's Sunday school class I taught at Bethel Baptist Church, Galesburg, Illinois, who cheered me on along the way and inspired me to study harder and communicate more effectively.

My pastors, *Lee Johnson* and *Kirk Kendall,* who know more about God than anyone I've met and maintain a grace-filled spirit in their leadership.

Chip MacGregor, literary agent and friend, who gets credit for sending the E-mail that sparked this entire book idea and continues to amaze me with his ability to make me laugh and think deep, sometimes at the same time.

Ramona Cramer Tucker—THE fastest editor on the face of the earth! You "hear" my writing voice over the scream of grammatical errors and my propensity to type "*;*" whenever there's a blank space.

Tammy Faxel, Carla Mayer, Janelle Howard, Jennifer Leo, and the token male, *Travis Thrasher,* who make up the fantastic (and fun!) team of Acquisitions, Marketing, and Author Relations at Tyndale House Publishers.

My writing girlfriends, *Cynthia Spell Humbert* and *Gracie Malone*— you can *always* be counted on to lift my spirits when I'm looking at a twenty-three-page pamphlet rather than a two-hundred-page manuscript and am convinced I know nothing and should go back to doing my family's laundry.

Donna Wallace—some people would say it was just a coincidence that we met that summer at CBA, but I know different. Whether you know this or not, *Scandalous* wouldn't have been its sassy self without your initial challenge to continue writing real.

*Listen to your life. See it for the fathomless mystery
that it is. In the boredom and pain of it no less than in the
excitement and gladness: touch, taste, smell your way to the holy
and hidden heart of it because in the last analysis all moments
are key moments, and life itself is grace.*[1]
Frederick Buechner

**This is the journey of scandalous grace,
scandalous living. . . .**

✳ 1 ✳

You Go, Gurrlfriend!

Well, here we are. Just you and me. Woman to woman. Chick to chick. Hormonally challenged to hormonally challenged! I've been waiting to talk with you for months. Years even.

We're more alike than you may realize. You don't believe me? Well, let me offer up the Gurrlfriend Hanky-Wave Test and see how you score. The first thing you have to do is grab a hanky. Now, I realize that if you did not grow up watching your father blow his nose into a neatly ironed white handkerchief and then stuff it back into his neatly pressed dress slacks, you may be unfamiliar with the term *hanky.* If so, consider yourself blessed . . . and be sure to write the manufacturers of Kleenex a note of thanks after reading this book.

But I digress. Just grab a hanky or something akin to it. A Kleenex, paper towel, or even your bra will do. Simply grab *something* and get ready to test your girlfriend knowledge.

Okay, now you have to assume the hanky-wave position. Do not fear! This demands nothing of you physically. You just gotta give me a little *at-ti-tude.* And I *know* you've got plenty of that. See if you can find something to weight the pages of this book down. I'd really like you to stand for a moment. . . .

Good. Now bend your right knee just a little. Keep the left leg a bit straighter. Put your wavin' hand in the air with your "hanky" of choice and the other hand on your hip. Now give me a little hip action, girlfriend, and wave that hanky a bit. And as you're doing this you'll want to add a little "That's right" action to your neck and head.

Attitude. It's all in the attitude.

If you can't seem to get the hips, hands, arms, and head going, just visualize the stance you might take if, after instructing your two-year-old son to stop some annoying habit in the center aisle of a jam-packed Target store, he bellows, "No, you silly old pooh-pooh head!"

That's what I thought. Now you've got the body language down pat.

It doesn't matter if you've borne a child or not. *Every* woman instinctively assumes the *Gurrlfriend–at-ti-tude* position when threatened by a two-foot terror.

All right, you are ready to go. I'm going to throw out a few statements and observations. If you can relate to them in any way whatsoever, give me a hanky wave.

* If you have ever enjoyed a bowl of ice cream that was so good you just had to lick the bowl—give me a hanky wave. *(In the Midwest it's Edy's Grand Cookie Dough. Enough said.)*
* If you grew up in a time when there was never any reason to question Bert and Ernie's living arrangements—give me a wholesome hanky wave.

✳ If you've walked into your parents' house and it just felt good—wave that hanky.

✳ If you believe all forms of control-top panty hose should be banned—give me a hanky wave.

See, here's the deal. Women who "need" control tops do not benefit in any way from the control. All these tortuous items manage to do is push your extra flesh up and over the waistband of said hosiery, thereby creating the ever envious and ever attractive inner tube of truth around the circumference of your waist. Just say NO to control tops.

✳ If you have ever asked someone, "When's your baby due?" and she was not pregnant—wave that hanky.

✳ If *you* have ever been asked, "When's your baby due?" and you were not pregnant—wave your hanky. *(I don't know which one is more painful! Here's some free advice: Assume everyone is carrying a little extra weight and NEVER ask this question.)*

✳ If you lie down at night and have a million thoughts—wave the hanky.

✳ If you have ever kissed a man so passionately that you never wanted it to end—well, give it up, girlfriend, and proudly wave that hanky.

✳ If you long to be a woman of integrity, a woman of spiritual substance . . . so much that you're going to memorize the Bible from Genesis to Maps, including knowing where the Old Testament book of Habakkuk is located—in fact, you'll gain so much knowledge that Kay Arthur is going to call YOU for teaching advice!—well, wave that hanky.

✳ If you have ever fallen asleep while praying . . . .
. . . . . ᴢᴢᴢᴢᴢᴢᴢᴢᴢᴢᴢᴢᴢᴢᴢᴢᴢᴢᴢᴢᴢ.

If this is YOU, then you, like me, need a lavish dose of God's scandalous grace. And that's exactly what this book is about. You see, "he wanted us to enter into the celebration of his lavish gift-giving by the hand of his beloved Son,"[2] because he knew of our need for it long before we ever did. I believe passionately this divine grace is for those who aren't perfect *(I'm waving my hanky)* and for those who may feel they are a grave disappointment to God and others because of their weight, lack of talent, mental acuity, sexual mishaps, and stubbornness *(I waved my hanky more than a time or two on that one).*

This book is written by a woman just like you. And, more than anything, I hope somewhere between this first chapter and the endnotes you come to regard me as a friend. *Your* friend, who wants nothing more than to talk with you about what scandalous grace is and why you and I so desperately need it.

It's all about wrapping our minds around the preposterous nature of God's grace, embracing it for ourselves, and then extending it to those around us.

Scandalously His,
Julie Ann Barnhill

* 2 *

I am Woman, Hear Me Roar!

I am a complex XX chromosome package of estrogen and water retention, prone to emotional overeating, impulse buying, and PMS jags that have been known to terrify grown men (mostly my husband) and unhousebroken pets.

I am a real woman living in the real world who, regardless of her thirty-something age status, still "peels out" on gravel, eats chocolate-chip cookie dough made with real eggs *(life is too short to mess with Egg Beaters)*, and routinely chauffeurs three mortified children around town in a beat-up 1990 Chevy Lumina minivan while belting out "Do You Believe In Love" with the one and only Huey Lewis and the News accompanying her on tape.

I believe in God, America, and the power of cheese.

My favorite color is red. I hate the color beige (more on this later) and someday I'm going to learn how to dance. I mean really dance.

I detest cauliflower and asparagus and have never forced my children to eat either of them "because they're good for you." I have, however, engaged in a ferocious battle of wills with my second child over macaroni and cheese.

One evening this child insisted (whined, fussed, begged, pleaded) that I make him a special order of said pasta for supper. I did. This child then refused to eat it and requested (whined, fussed, begged, pleaded) another food item. Setting his dinner plate in front of him, I said, "No, you're going to eat this macaroni and cheese because you asked for macaroni and cheese. *Capich?*"

He no understand.

I translated, "You'll sit here until you eat the macaroni."

Four hours later I wrapped the macaroni with Cling Wrap, tucked the delinquent into bed, and whispered in his ear, "I guess you'll be having cold mac and cheese for breakfast, because one way or another you're going to eat what you asked for." Eight hours later he consumed said food item—then promptly threw up at the table.

I found out later that his school served macaroni and cheese for lunch that day. Is there an odd sense of justice in this world for mothers or what?

✳ ✳ ✳

It was my thirtieth birthday—July 21, 1995—when I embraced real living. As I was sitting in my living room, giving my baby a bottle, suddenly the sky opened, a trumpet sounded, and I heard, "Julie, get real with your life."

Okay, so it was the screen door that opened and my six-year-old daughter trumpeting, "Mommy, Ricky's going potty in the front yard again," but it was profound nevertheless.

"Time's a wastin'," my grandmother used to say, and this

time I chose to listen. So on that day honoring my birth I started doing a little "real life, real time" housecleaning.

Hence my refusing to wear panty hose or slips ever again. (Even upon threat of being written out of the family will by my undergarment-lovin' mother.) And as a result of a reduction procedure (I'll talk about that later, and the transforming effects it had on my self-esteem and my life in general, so stay posted), I am forever free from the confines of a much-detested twelve-hook brassiere. *(You're shocked, aren't you? You had no idea good Christian women walk around without bras on!)*

I did, however, purchase a *shaper* in hopes that my hips might acclimate themselves back to their 1982 position. My husband mistakenly referred to it as a girdle. He committed this error in judgment *once*. Trust me; you don't want to know the details.

I also made a list of "basement" people in my life. You know, those folks who have a talent for making you feel miserable or inferior . . . usually both. Well, I made that list and began to repeat these words daily: "I only have so many hours in my day and I choose not to spend them with you." Now I know that may sound cold-blooded, and I didn't say those exact words to my cellar-loving acquaintances, but I did start drawing some boundaries, including limiting the time I spent with them. It was freeing, I tell you, and it felt marvelous.

I am woman, hear me roar!

But I'm also living, breathing proof of what's troubling real women everywhere.

It seems I am never quite settled with what I have. Always reaching . . . stretching . . . yearning . . . for what lies just beyond my grasp, I find myself longing for more.

More oomph in my life. More zest in my zing. More zip in my do-dah! But more times than not, the only Zest I get zinged with is a shower soap that finds its way into my eyes and leaves me partially blinded for six hours or so.

Honestly, some days I've concluded that it's just not worth getting out of bed.

I think it's important for you to know these things about me. After all, we're going to be spending a decent amount of time with each other in this book. I figure it's always nice to know who you're dealing with and to be able to answer this question: "Is this woman insane?"

Rest assured, I am not.

I'm just a woman living in a real world of laundry, work deadlines, past-due mortgage payments, dysfunctional interpersonal relationships, and "I want my 1982 hips back!" shaper issues.

I am also a *real woman of faith* who finds the road to heaven paved with frustration, doubt, faithlessness, niggling sins, panic, angst, and the need for confession . . . over and over and over again.

And, I suppose, as a result of my doubting, my faithlessness, and my propensity to sin, I find myself grappling with a crazy little thing called *grace:* grace that understands my doubting. Grace that carries me through unbelief and tenderly deals with my faithless heart. Grace that neither ignores nor condemns my struggle with disobedience. Divine grace that assures me (and you), "My grace is enough; it's all you need. My strength comes into its own in your weakness."[3]

Grace, grace, God's grace . . . *that's* what I long to understand and know. And I'm guessing that if you picked up this book, you do too.

As I've spoken to tens of thousands of women across the country and reached millions via media spots on the *Oprah Winfrey Show,* NBC's *The Other Half* with Dick Clark, and *CNN World News,* I have found that no matter where we may live or what our social or economic status may be, we all long for similar things.

Time and time again, while sequestered in a convention meeting room, waiting at a crowded security checkpoint in an airport, or talking over the telephone or by E-mail, I've found myself engaging in thoughtful and passionate conversations with women. We never remain strangers for long, as they trust me with their dreams, their failures, and the desire for living a life that is "real." As I've chatted with them, I've realized something significant: We women want to stop playing games and deal with the things that trouble us the most—and if we can keep our sanity in the process, all the better.

✳ ✳ ✳

The realization that we women long for transformed lives became even more clear to me one day as I was shuffling along the narrow aisle of American Airlines Flight 2803, trying hard not to inflict bodily harm on some poor unsuspecting passenger. The ridiculously overstuffed carry-on slung across my shoulder *(it could have been mistaken for a microwave)* was bursting at its faux-leather seams. Travel notes, magazines, cell phone, walking shoes, half-eaten candy bars, a three-day-old bottle of tepid spring water, my Palm Pilot, and participant responses from an event I had just keynoted all threatened to explode from their pregnant confines.

I finally came to window seat 14A. Heaving the carry-on straight above my head, I attempted to place it into the small overhead compartment. It didn't place. I then attempted what's commonly referred to as the "shove and wiggle," hoping to coax the bag into place. All I managed to garner was an appreciative glance from an elderly gentleman seated near me and grunts of impatience from the 14B passenger and the higher-seat-number crowd lined up behind me.

Desperate times call for desperate measures, wouldn't you agree?

Bench-pressing that monstrosity one more time over my head, I nudged it as far as possible on the overhead lip. Then I climbed on the seat adjacent to me, locked my knees, and shoved that puppy like nobody's business. Just as I felt it begin to move and was starting to inwardly cheer, an outside clasp on the bag broke loose and showered the now mutinous passengers around me in an avalanche of loose-leaf paper.

The skies of flying were anything but friendly at that particular moment.

I gave up. Yanking the bag out and away from the overhead, I stepped down, made a mad dash for a large majority of the paper at my feet, and then slithered back to 14A. Somehow managing to collect the remaining scattered papers from the few passengers still willing to acknowledge my existence, I then considered—briefly—hanging myself with the seat belt. Instead I elected to snap it snuggly against my hips and then melted into a pool of humiliation.

Anxious to look busy, as to dissuade anyone who might feel led to smack me, I began sorting through the hodgepodge of paperwork on my lap.

All thoughts concerning the spectacle I had just made subsided as I began to read the responses to a question I had posed days earlier at a women's conference. The weekend had centered on the subject of God's scandalous grace for women and finding the strength to "let it go" concerning areas of specific pain and struggle in our lives. Handing out lined notebook paper to all participants, I asked them to share with me their greatest fears and spiritual disappointments as women. Here are a few of their responses.

✳ The fear of not measuring up to everyone's expectations—including God's.

✳ My thinking, *If I could just be obedient in that area.* I'm so afraid I won't ever be able to be obedient.

✳ Believing everything needs to be perfect—especially with my kids.

✳ Disappointment in my relationship with my sister.

✳ My long absence from a church and doubting if Jesus still wants and loves me.

✳ The fear of making a mistake and not pleasing God.

✳ My adult child.

✳ Material things—I'm too possessive and freak out if my children lose something.

✳ My struggle with God's will versus my desire.

✳ Anger toward my husband.

✳ My addiction to food.

✳ Guilt for my horrible language—I've been a Christian for so long but still talk this way. (Maybe I don't trust God enough.)

✳ Money issues. Always money issues.

✳ My fear of interacting with other women.

✳ Wanting to be thin.

✳ The fact that I could love my mother-in-law if she would just communicate with me and appreciate what I do for her.

✳ Some of the hurtful things my husband said or did in the early years of our marriage. I say I forgive but I can't let it go.

✳ A habit my husband has that just eats at me. I almost feel hatred toward him when I see him do it. Is that sad or what, Julie?

✳ Being critical of the way people in charge run their programs. It bothers me that others can't see a better way of doing things that would save them time, money, and problems.

✳ Thinking I'm not committed enough to God.

✳ I can't let go of the disappointment of a broken engagement.

✳ Fear of losing friends if they really knew everything about me.

✳ Holding back on letting people into my space. I'm a loner and would like God to change my feelings toward myself. I'd love to believe that I am an adequate human being—capable of God's and other people's love. But it's just so hard to believe that, especially about myself.

Read through those confessions again.

Each one resonates—finds a home, so to speak—with my own longings for acceptance, love, refreshment, and release. Thousands of us *(dare I write millions of us?)* can understand the female souls that question God's love for them. Many of us wonder, often in silence, if, in our aimless wanderings and frail human failings we have forever breached a holy line of demarcation, resulting in our disqualification from ever experiencing the extravagant realities of this thing called *grace*.

And so you find me.

A woman of faith implicitly believing there is more. More to be known, understood, and embraced concerning God and his love for me—for us. More to life and more to this active organism of scandalous grace than my routine prayers, impassioned spiritual utterances, or ethereal wonderings have ever fathomed.

And so we find ourselves.

Each intrinsically yearning for Grand Canyon grace.

Forget the "small fries" lessons you heard about during a sleepy Sunday school class or annual Lent service—you have to think bigger, deeper, and wider. Let it go and "Super Size" your thoughts—because true grace, *divine grace,* is nothing if not lavish.

✳ ✳ ✳

When I think of the word *lavish,* I always think of my grandmother. When I was a child, I loved to watch my grandma prepare her homemade angel food cake—a cake that required thirteen egg whites. Gently cracking each porcelain-white shell, she'd separate whites from yolk, back and forth, with almost hypnotic ease—one half shell to the other with nary a drop co-mingling. Grabbing a wire whisk, she would then beat whites, sugar, vanilla, cream of tartar, and a pinch of salt into a frothy melee of stiff peaks. Soon enough, after gently folding the dry ingredients into a smooth mix, she would pour the foamy white batter into a tube cake pan, carefully place it in the oven, and leave it alone.

No opening the door to "check."

No harsh movements or wild stomping. *(Heaven help the rambunctious grandchild who played a role in its airy demise.)*

Upon cooling, Grandma would gingerly invert it onto a glass pedestal stand and gently shake it free from its moorings.

And there it stood—a ten-inch-high testament to angel food cake perfection. Her job was almost complete, save for the frosting. Grandma would then request, "Two bricks of cheese, please"—bricks being eight-ounce portions of Philadelphia brand cream cheese, softened at room temperature. She would combine those bricks with half-and-half, pure vanilla, powdered sugar, and, just in case a fat gram could go unanswered, a dollop of Land O' Lakes salted, pure cream butter. Then she'd beat the entire bowl of ingredients until they were a creamy delight.

One swift stroke of her spatula, and *plop*—a tantalizing portion of icing was dropped and then drawn across the canvas of the cake. Another stroke, another portion—*plop*. Time and time again, with the artistry of Michelangelo, her unrestrained use of artery-blocking, cholesterol-loving ingredients morphed into an exquisite exclamation point of confectionary grace upon the cake.

It was a *coup de grâce,* that cake! I mean, who deserves not one but *two* bricks of soft cream cheese, vanilla, powdered sugar, and pure cream butter?

So too the decisive stroke—the audacious act of the Divine that made possible the lavish application of grace in our lives. For Jesus' act of sacrifice is a grace that crossed eternity—an exquisite grace that made the Way for you and me, real women with baggage and "issues," to know the pleasures of mercy and forgiveness. And it is this grace alone that can restore the vitality of our souls, our bodies, and our minds—vitality that otherwise will lie dormant and wasted in recessed corners of our existence.

Coup de *scandalous* grace severed *all* rules of Supreme Being propriety and introduced a loving and gracious Father, ready to bend near with compassion toward a world fraught with humanity's failings and mistakes. It introduced a Divine Parent ready to meet each and every one of us right where we are and to introduce us to freedom and revolution for our thoughts and actions, and healing for the most messed-up places in our lives.

For if we live life at all, we will have "messed-up" places to contend with.

May I just say something and get it out into the open? We're *all* dysfunctional. There isn't one of us who hasn't "functioned abnormally" at some point in time. There isn't one of us who has skated through life without an impairment of some sort tagging behind her. As graphic artist Mary Engelbreit exhorts in her drawings, "Let's put the FUN back in dysfunctional!"

Listen: I struggle. I dream. I aspire to be more like Jesus.

And on other days? Well, I think I'm as much like him as I care to be.

Ah, such is the marvelous journey of life.

I am convinced that most women could stand a heaping dose of scandalous grace that enables them to cut themselves—as well as one another—some serious slack. *Let it go* slack toward the "sistah" relationships—the *Ya-Ya* women in one's life. Mothers, friends, daughters, socialites, professionals, and scholars, as well as those once-in-a-lifetime encounters we have with complete strangers—women we come across while traveling through Chicago's O'Hare International Airport, cashiers at out-of-state vacation stops, and countless others.

It is *this* grace, unrestrained and unrelenting, that I must possess, for my soul thirsts for refreshment in the scorched and dry places of my being. It is this grace, exorbitant and over-the-top, that truly becomes "the icing on the cake" of life—freeing us as women and provoking us to live outwardly with mercy and forgiveness toward one another and ourselves.

I'm reminded of a wonderful line found in Brennan Manning's book, *The Ragamuffin Gospel*: "Beggars know how to open their hands, trusting that the crumb of grace will fall."

The crumb of grace.

How audacious.

The crumb of scandalous grace did not speak a harsh word to the naked, fearful, and shamed woman caught in the act of adultery (read this powerful story for yourself in John, chapter 8). Rather, grace demonstrated gentleness, compassion, and divine forgiveness.

How extravagant.

The crumb of scandalous grace forgives and covers my petty, self-serving, self-absorbed ways and helps reveal the woman beneath their shallow veneer—a woman unashamed to beg, *yet again,* for more of the divine.

How life-transforming!

The crumb of scandalous grace brings both eternal and internal life to those bold enough to ask.

How exquisite, indeed!

On my own journey I have learned that mere crumbs of God's grace are sufficient to fill a hungry soul. May this book be instrumental in your discovering the liberating A–to–Z grace available to carry you as a woman! Grace that leaves you deeply rooted in him. Grace that leaves you well constructed upon him. And grace that empowers you to start living it in and through, about and over, above and under, all things that come your way.[4]

Divine grace beckons us as women to both hunger and thirst, bringing a depth and richness to our lives. *Scandalous grace* calls to us with brazen promise, "Take all you want, because there's plenty more where that came from!"

* 3 *

GRACE IN THE REAL WORLD

Hers isn't an uncommon story, not by today's standards.

An unmarried woman has a one-time sexual encounter with a man, a man who is physically and emotionally available during a time of great stress in her life. And one who finds her attractive and desirable.

They sleep together.

More pointedly stated, but far closer to the truth, she says, they experience sexual climax and lie side by side in an odd, uncomfortable silence for a few hours. Then, self-consciously gathering her clothes, she says good-bye and closes his apartment door behind her.

Good-bye.

No "I'll call you later," or "Where do we go from here?"

You see, before they got together, she had understood (and accepted) that this "thing" they had was sex—pure and simple. Sex that had temporarily sated an immediate need to forget problems and tangled frustrations. Sex seemingly without guilt or relational responsibility. Just plain, old 1990s "I'll have forgotten all about this in three days" sex.

Six weeks and three days passed. During that time Jason, a former boyfriend, contacted her and asked if they could spend some time together. He wanted to reconnect with her, he said, to see if something was still there—a spark between them that they could rekindle.

So she agreed to meet him at his parents' home. As she hung up the phone, a tentative smile flitted across her face. She had liked Jason so much when they were dating! Allowing herself to hope, if only a little, she played out their reunion. She had always been so comfortable around Jason. He was physically attractive, oh yes, but more than that, he was kind.

Why had they broken up in the first place? She couldn't remember now. Shrugging, she admitted (but only to herself) that in all likelihood the breakup had been her idea. For whatever reasons, the very attributes—kindness, friendship, and loyalty—she now longed to share with a man were the very things she had found bothersome about Jason in the past.

Did I throw away the best thing that ever happened to me? she wondered. If so, she wasn't going to make that same mistake again.

So with a crazy mix of apprehension and longing, she counted down the days until she was to drive to his childhood home.

She never anticipated what was to come.

On the day she was supposed to travel, she didn't feel well. In fact, she hadn't felt well for several days. Fatigue seemed to envelop her body and mind from the moment she awakened. She thought about calling Jason and canceling, but her heart screamed at her to go. As she drove, mile after mile, she began to feel worse.

When at last she saw the familiar home of Jason's parents, her body collapsed in relief. To her horror, she barely uttered a greeting before she found herself bent over a cold toilet bowl, dry heaves riding over her body, sending her into convulsive fits of nonproductive vomiting. For what seemed to be hours, nausea hit her again and again. Wave upon wave of sickness literally brought her to her knees and left her spent and haggard.

This was certainly not what she had planned. For this day . . . or for her life.

Years later she would learn that Jason thought she had cancer or some equally horrific disease. He had believed she was dying. What else could account for the strange guttural noises coming from the bathroom?

Well, she felt like she was dying on that day, but she knew she wasn't suffering from some unknown disease or terminal illness. She knew it wasn't "You only have *X* number of days to live" dramatic, or even terminal, for that matter. All she had to do was count back six weeks and three days and see herself—in bed, with a man, unknowingly creating life.

She was pregnant—and drowning in fear and shame.

That weekend, unable to explain her illness to Jason or the cold emotional front she constructed to protect her heart, she drove away from his home hours before she had planned.

She couldn't find the strength to contact the father of the baby either. Even if she did, she was fairly certain he wouldn't care.

So she simply dealt with it by herself. She berated herself and wondered, *How could I have been so stupid?* After all, she called herself a Christian. She knew all the rules, as well as the dos and don'ts of premarital sex. She had attempted "love can wait," on more than one occasion. *Only one time when I didn't wait,* she thought. *And look where I ended up—unmarried, pregnant, and alone.*

So she carried the weight by herself, for as long as she could. Finally *(you knew that would come, didn't you? For we all finally reach a point where we can't carry our burdens alone),* she had had enough.

About two weeks after her visit to Jason's parents' house, she decided to tell him. He had continued to call and write—making it abundantly clear that he wanted her to be a part of his life. Worse, she wanted that too, but she just couldn't see it happening once he found out about the baby.

One cool May morning she called him, and they arranged to meet at one of their favorite outdoor places.

Years later, as she was telling me this poignant true tale, she said, "I don't suppose there's a *good* way to tell your *almost* boyfriend that you're pregnant with someone else's baby. But I owed it to Jason to hear it from me first and to let him know I understood why he'd want to end our relationship."

And so she decided to tell the truth, as hard as it was. Even when she was certain what the consequences would be—losing Jason forever.

Sitting on a bright yellow blanket near the shore of a quiet lake, she looked at Jason and said, "I spent the night with a man one time, and now I'm pregnant with his baby."

She held her breath as she watched Jason, awaiting his reaction. Would it be cursing, accusations, disgust, anger, betrayal, repulsion, outrage? Then she was perplexed. She detected what appeared to be compassion veiling his eyes and expression.

Compassion? This empathetic possibility had never crossed her mind. Was it truly possible? Did she really see tenderness in his eyes?

He drew her into his arms and quietly asked, "Do you love him?"

That's all.

Nothing else.

Just, "Do you love him?"

She lay against his chest and exhaled, relaxing for perhaps the first time in eight weeks. Listening to the steady rhythm of his beating heart, she answered, "No, I don't love him."

Drawing her tighter, enfolding her in intoxicating security and acceptance, he then kissed the top of her head and whispered, "I'm here for you, no matter what that brings—I'm here."

And it was "here" she broke down.

"But I don't deser—" She tried to speak through her tears.

But he wouldn't allow it. Pressing his lips against hers, he kissed her and shushed her. Then he held her even closer. "I'm here," is all he said. "I'm here." And he said it over and over again until at last she fell asleep in the comforting arms of scandalous grace.*

How often have we expressed to others, and perhaps God himself, "But I don't deserve . . ."?

After all I've done . . . I don't deserve forgiveness.

After all I've said . . . I don't deserve mercy.

---

*They have been married for ten years now—a family of three built upon the unshakable foundation of scandalous and preposterous grace.

After all I've believed . . . I don't deserve understanding.
After all . . .

I find myself observing the women who come in and out of my life—their interactions with one another, their comments about faith and life—and sense that they too grapple with the spiritual concept of grace directed *toward* them.

Why is it so difficult for women (myself included) to embrace the idea of a divine grace that forgives without end? Why do we shy away from the concept of a divine grace that is able to restore the very things we have given up as lost and irreparably damaged? Why do we cower from divine grace that spills, without measure, into our hearts and lives? Grace that can cover—without fail—our mistakes, our errors, our flagrant misdeeds and secret sins?

Perhaps we struggle with such grace because we've not allowed ourselves to voice our deepest need and longing for such soul refreshment. Perhaps we dare not trust grace, *this* divine grace, because we are afraid to voice our desperate need for it. Perhaps we cower, for we have yet to embrace the magnanimous truth regarding our sin and his ability to forgive. After all, "sin didn't, and doesn't, have a chance in competition with the aggressive forgiveness we call *grace.* When it's sin versus grace, grace wins hands down."[5]

The term *scandalous grace* oozes into the territory of the forbidden, the shocking, the out-of-bounds. In nearly every circumstance in which I have shared the premise for this book's subject, it has raised the eyebrows of the woman I'm speaking to and caused her to say, "Oh, that sounds interesting! Tell me *more* about that kind of grace!"

Scandalous grace is not a subject for the faint of heart. It is a matter of epic and gloriously emotional proportions. It cannot be encapsulated into one neat and tidy paragraph. In fact, it is anything *but* neat and tidy. And no matter how many books are written on the subject, well, there will always be more to say. Thus, the need for the book you hold in your hands!

* * *

Scandalous grace is wild. Untamed. It breaks all the rules. It possesses seemingly contradictory meanings. *Merriam-Webster's Collegiate Dictionary* defines *scandalous* as "offensive to propriety or morality" and *grace* as "a virtue coming from God." What a dichotomy this seems to present! For to go against "propriety" is to go against the Miss Manners school of proper behavior or appropriate action.

Look at it this way. We all know not to pick our nose in public. That goes against proper behavior. Many of us learned at an early age that it's "improper" to stare at someone or make loud comments about another's dress or appearance. We learned, oftentimes without a word being spoken, the "appropriate" way to go about things. And *appropriate* oftentimes comes with a boatload of dos and don'ts.

And then you meet a dropout of Miss Manners training.

She talks too much—and way too honestly.

She laughs too loud—and at the goofiest things.

She hangs out with misfits—and seems to fit in a little too well.

She dives into life—and you're convinced she'll drown as a result.

And all the "dos and don'ts" protocols that everyone else seems to recognize and abide by? Well, she seems to take special delight in breaking each and every one of them.

That's exactly what *scandalous divine grace* does. It goes against protocol and conventional appropriateness. It doesn't "bend" the rules but scripts entirely new ones! Like these:

> Love those who have never shown love to you.
> Don't get revenge, even when you can.
> Think of others before yourself.
> Forgive time and time . . . and time again.
> Think of the eternal in all of the earthly.
> Give without thought of the cost.

Such grace sweeps across our lives. It splatters the safe, beige canvases of our existence with chartreuse brush strokes of the divine! It infuses our days and nights, months and years, with riotous possibility!

Here's what I have found to be true: Divine grace encompasses more—so much more—than the carefully bound and autopsied facts and experiences we may have closeted somewhere far away in our hearts and minds. Scandalous grace breaks through and implodes our life and our relationships. It heals our soul, mends our heart, challenges our thoughts, and equips us to deal with the physical, sexual, and spiritual realities of being female.

We need such grace, girlfriends! Grace for our lives, and grace to dispense the same to those in our lives. In order to grasp the veracity of such grace myself, I came up with this alphabetical primer. Maybe it will help you too!

Scandalous grace is . . .

Audacious: intrepidly daring; marked by originality
and verve

Bold: standing out prominently

Commodious: roomy and comfortable

Dazzling: causing amazement

Exorbitant: exceeding in intensity, quality, amount, or size
of the customary or appropriate limits

Fiery: full of or exuding emotion or spirit

Genuine: authentic; real

Heartwarming: cheery

Intimate: marked by a warm friendship developing through
long association

Judicious: wise; thoughtful

Kooky: deviating from conventional or accepted usage or
conduct, especially in odd or whimsical ways

Liberating: free from domination

Meticulous: detailed

Necessary: absolutely needed

Out-of-Bounds: outside the prescribed boundaries or limits

Preposterous: contrary to nature, reason, or common
sense

Quenching: satisfying

Radiant: marked by or expressive of love, confidence, or
happiness

Sacred: holy; blessed

Transforming: changing completely

Unrestrained: free of constraint

Veracious: truthful

Wanton: extravagant

Xquisite: intense

Yielded: accommodating

Zealous: enthusiastic

None of us deserve such grace. And most of us well know that. None of us have earned the right to such grace. But oh, how we've tried! Our receiving or experiencing such grace is solely contingent upon, rooted in, and thoroughly grounded upon, the very character and nature of God. And as such, scandalous grace brings both *eternal* and *internal* life to every woman who will ask and receive. Life that is able to live with abandon. Life that is satisfied. And life that dares to take the road less traveled.

The scandal of divine grace encompasses our salvation, our desires. It covers the here and now of living with our mistakes and failures. It sweeps across the canvas of our lives and speaks to women who are restless in Seattle—as well as Anaheim, Kansas City, Durango, Baltimore, Tucson, Atlanta, or wherever you call home.

4

Stomach Girl

$\mathcal{J}$t was maybe a year ago when I found myself at Atlanta's Hartsfield International Airport in the Peach State of Georgia with a four-hour unscheduled layover.

I had managed to entertain myself for an hour with a Philly cheese steak sandwich, as well as a scoop of Ben & Jerry's mint-chocolate-chunk ice cream. But with three hours remaining, I proceeded to haul my faux-leather carry-on *(same small tote mentioned previously)* through the WHSmith bookstore.

Maybe it was the suspicious size of my bag. Or the eight hardback books I managed to knock from their display. But I got the distinct impression *(security following behind me, speaking in hushed tones)* that I wasn't welcome in that shop. I can take a hint, so I made my way to the ladies' rest room.

As I walked through the entrance, two older women came in behind me. Laughing comfortably with each other, they began to "talk shop." Grandchildren, retirement funds, bunion surgery, plans for the holidays—you name it, they dished it. I waited for an available stall as they made their way to the heavily lit, mirrored vanity.

I had just locked the door in front of me when I overheard one of them say, "Honestly, Helen, would you just take a look at my stomach in these pants!"

I voyeuristically peeked through the gap between the stall wall and door and observed Stomach Girl and her friend Helen.

Stomach Girl continued. "I mean, really, it looks just awful in these pants!" She then began to pat herself down, as we women are wont to do when it comes to bulging areas on our bodies, somehow believing this will smooth away any problem areas. She turned this way and that. Sucked her stomach muscles in. Let her stomach muscles out. Pulled her shirt out of her waistband and knotted it. Tucked her shirt back into her waistband.

Back and forth she went, on and on gazing at her reflection in the mirror. Until, finally, Helen could stand it no longer. Looking directly into the eyes of her seemingly dear friend, she admonished, "Oh, please, June! *You* look perfectly fine in those pants. *Your stomach* looks fine in those pants. I don't know what you're complaining about, anyway."

Pregnant pause.

Then Helen added, "If you want to see a really awful stomach, just take a look at mine."

And then, to my voyeuristic horror, Helen pulled down *her* waistband and Haines and let us all take a gander.

June looked at Helen. Helen looked at June. I passed out. *(Trust me, it's hard to argue with a couple of C-sections and a 1960s-era gallbladder scar.)*

Waving a white flag of surrender, June finally responded, "Well, I guess. Your stomach *is* worse than mine." Then she gazed at her reflection in the mirror one more time and muttered with heavy resignation to no one in particular I could just lose ten pounds and flatten it up a bit—*everything* would be a lot better."

Are you familiar with the famous Edvard Munch painting titled *The Scream*? Well, that's exactly how my face looked in that cold, gray-tiled bathroom stall in Atlanta. Mouth open, hands to my face, agonized mental wailings that sounded something like this: "Auurrrggggghhhhh!"

I believe it was at this precise juncture that I began pounding my head against the stainless steel sanitary napkin holder.

Perhaps you are scratching your head, wondering what exactly brought on such a passionate (and rather painful) reaction from me to the above statement. So allow me to put the last piece of the puzzle together for you . . . June and Helen had to be pushing eighty-five years of age.

Someone stop the insanity!

Think about it.

June honestly thought ten pounds was going to make all the difference in the world. And I'd be willing to bet that the same little ditty had crossed her mind on more than one occasion during her lifetime.

Just as that same little ditty crosses my mind at thirty-seven years old, except it's closer to *twenty-five* pounds that's going to change my life.

And I do mean CHANGE MY LIFE.

✳ Twenty-five pounds, and I'll feel more confident in public, thereby insuring an elusive something that I don't seem to have preweight loss. As Bono of U2 once sang, "I still haven't found what I'm looking for . . ." but I'm pretty sure it's hiding under those twenty-five pounds.

✳ Twenty-five pounds, and I'll be able to fit into a pair of sassy leather pants that I've been pining for since 1982.

✳ Twenty-five pounds, and I'll be asked to host a national television talk show.

✳ Twenty-five pounds, a flatter stomach, and . . . *(say it with me, girls)* . . . "everything will be better."

Crazy, huh? Crazy as my Peeping-Tom status behind a locked stall. Crazy as my watching Helen and June gather their things and walk out into a world where octogenarian-age women *still* obsess over an elusive and blasted ten pounds of perfection.

Ten pounds flatter, and everything will be better.

As if.

I know I'm not the only woman asking the question, "Doesn't it ever end?"

I mean, really. I was kind of hoping by age eighty-something that I would be able to look over my life and consider the fact that I had survived economic depressions, made it through wars and rumors of war, given birth to children, raised them, watched grandchildren tackle their future, and somehow have something to talk about *other* than the size of my stomach.

But the reality of living life in the real world is this: We all have our limits on what we think grace covers. Be it a pregnancy before marriage, weight-loss struggles that never seem to end, or any number of mistakes and regrets—most of us are holding on to something that we cannot imagine others, let alone God, can forgive or accept as part of us.

There's a familiar parable told about a wayward son and his faithful father. Author Philip Yancey rewrote it as a modern parable in his book *What's So Amazing About Grace?* I include it here because it reveals the scandalous nature of grace at work.

A young girl grows up on a cherry orchard just above Traverse City, Michigan. Her parents, a bit old-fashioned, tend to overreact to her nose ring, the music she listens to, and the length of her skirts. They ground her a few times, and she seethes inside. "I hate you!" she screams at her father when he knocks on the door of her room after an argument, and that night she acts on a plan she has mentally rehearsed scores of times. She runs away.

She has visited Detroit only once before, on a bus trip with her church youth group to watch the Tigers play. Because newspapers in Traverse City report in lurid detail the gangs, the drugs, and the violence in downtown Detroit, she concludes that is probably the last place her parents will look for her. California, maybe, or Florida, but not Detroit.

Her second day there she meets a man who drives the biggest car she's ever seen. He offers her a ride, buys her lunch, and arranges a place for her to stay. He gives her pills that make her feel better than she's ever felt before. She was right all along, she decides: her parents were keeping her from all the fun.

The good life continues for a month, two months, a year. The man with the big car—she calls him "Boss"—teaches her a few things that men like. Since she's underage, men pay a premium for her. She lives in a penthouse, and orders room service whenever she wants. Occasionally she thinks about the folks back home, but their lives now seem so boring and provincial that she can hardly believe she grew up there.

She has a brief scare when she sees her picture printed on the back of a milk carton with the headline "Have you seen this child?" But by now she has blond hair, and with all the makeup and body-piercing jewelry she wears, nobody would mistake her for a child. Besides, most of her friends are runaways, and nobody squeals in Detroit.

After a year the first sallow signs of illness appear, and it amazes her how fast the boss turns mean. "These days, we can't mess around," he growls, and before she knows it she's out on the street without a penny to her name. She still turns a couple of tricks a night, but they don't pay much, and all the money goes to support her habit. When winter blows in she finds herself sleeping on metal grates outside the big department stores. "Sleeping" is the wrong word—a teenage girl at night in downtown Detroit can never relax her guard. Dark bands circle her eyes. Her cough worsens.

One night as she lies awake listening for footsteps, all of a sudden everything about her life looks different. She no longer feels like a woman of the world. She feels like a little girl, lost in a cold and frightening city. She begins to whimper. Her pockets are empty and she's hungry. She needs a fix. She pulls her legs tight underneath her and shivers under the newspapers she's piled atop her coat. Something jolts a synapse of memory and a single image fills her mind: of May in Traverse City, when a million cherry trees blossom at once, with her golden retriever dashing through the rows and rows of blossomy trees in chase of a tennis ball.

God, why did I leave, she says to herself, and pain stabs at her heart. *My dog back home eats better than I do now.* She's sobbing, and she knows in a flash that more than anything else in the world she wants to go home.

Three straight phone calls, three straight connections with the answering machine. She hangs up without leaving a message the first two times, but the third time she says, "Dad, Mom, it's me. I was wondering about maybe coming home. I'm catching a bus up your way, and it'll get there about midnight tomorrow. If you're not there, well, I guess I'll just stay on the bus until it hits Canada."

It takes about seven hours for a bus to make all the stops between Detroit and Traverse City, and during that time she realizes the flaws in her plan. What if her parents are out of town and miss the message? Shouldn't she have waited another day or so until she could talk to them? And even if they are home, they probably wrote her off as dead long ago. She should have given them some time to overcome the shock.

Her thoughts bounce back and forth between those worries and the speech she is preparing for her father.

"Dad, I'm sorry. I know I was wrong. It's not your fault; it's all mine. Dad, can you forgive me?" She says the words over and over, her throat tightening even as she rehearses them. She hasn't apologized to anyone for years.

The bus has been driving with lights on since Bay City. Tiny snowflakes hit the pavement rubbed worn by thousands of tires, and the asphalt steams. She's forgotten how dark it gets at night out here. A deer darts across the road and the bus swerves. Every so often, a billboard. A sign posting the mileage to Traverse City. *Oh, God.*

When the bus finally rolls into the station, its air brakes hissing in protest, the driver announces in a crackly voice over the microphone, "Fifteen minutes, folks, that's all we have here." Fifteen minutes to decide her life. She checks herself in a compact mirror, smooths her hair, and licks the lipstick off her teeth. She looks at the tobacco stains on her fingertips, and wonders if her parents will notice. If they're there.

She walks into the terminal not knowing what to expect. Not one of the thousand scenes that have played out in her mind prepare her for what she sees. There, in the concrete-walls-and-plastic-chairs bus terminal in Traverse City, Michigan, stands a group of forty brothers and sisters and great-aunts and uncles and cousins and a grandmother and great-grandmother to boot. They're all wearing goofy party hats and blowing noisemakers, and taped across the entire wall of the terminal is a computer-generated banner that reads, "Welcome home!"

Out of the crowd of well-wishers breaks her dad. She

stares out through the tears quivering in her eyes like hot mercury and begins the memorized speech, "Dad, I'm sorry. I know . . . "

He interrupts her. "Hush, child. We've no time for that. No time for apologies. You'll be late for the party. A banquet's waiting for you at home."[6]

How's that for breaking the rules of social propriety?

I have been drawn to this story time and time again because Yancey never fails to confront me with the preposterous nature of divine grace. Indeed, grace that forgives without measure, grace that hushes a wayward daughter, quiets an embarrassed and shamed pregnant woman, and restores relationships that were bent beyond repair . . . well, that is the epitome of preposterous—for all those actions are contrary to human nature, reason, or common sense.

Oh, how I yearn for the generous, healing grace of God! As a man named Paul wrote two thousand years ago, "He throws caution to the winds, giving to the needy in reckless abandon. His right-living, right-giving ways never run out, never wear out."[7]

God knew that I would come along—a needy woman who has, over the years, made quite a mess of things. God knows even now that I struggle to live out, in the daily grind of life, the things that come so easily off my tongue and keyboard strokes. God knows that I struggle with dark emotions of anger and bitterness—and that I long to be free from feelings of abandon-ment, shame, regret, and loneliness.

And he knew that you and I would doubt such grace exists. He knew we would rage, scream, and sulk. He knew all this as he formed us in our mother's womb (see Psalm 139:13-16).

Wombs that welcomed us.

Or wombs that wanted nothing to do with us once we were born.

He knew.

It is here I begin to melt. For I know what it's like to have a past you'd just as soon forget. A past that you had no control over—your family of origin; your mother's choice of lifestyle; your family's battle with alcohol—as well as a past of misgiv-ings made by your own free will.

I also know what it's like to hedge on the truth concerning your past. To hope against hope that it will remain hidden—secret—safely tucked away from public consumption.

But hiding from our past is never safe for our souls.

And so I have come to adopt a new philosophy for women like me. A confession of sorts that I encourage audiences to embrace and proclaim. As women hold hands all around the auditorium, I admit to one and all, "I am a mess." Generally they stare at me and then one another—wondering if I really said what they thought they heard. I assure them that I did indeed say, "I am a mess," and encourage them to repeat those four words aloud on the count of three. 1, 2, 3 . . . The first time generally invokes a tepid response at best and is almost always followed with a more enthusiastic declaration at my request.

I then go on to say, "Now, I don't believe in doing anything halfway. It's all or nothing in my life. So with that in mind, I proclaim to you that not only am I a mess . . . but I am a mess of magnificent proportions!" And with glee I lead them into proclaiming, "I am a mess of magnificent proportions." (Dramatic arm gestures are encouraged!)

Then I have them make eye contact with someone else and ask them to say, "You are a mess of magnificent proportions!"

Funny—I never have to encourage them to do this one with more vigor!

And while the laughter is subsiding I tell them, "That's why we need grace of magnificent proportions."

We all have "issues." We all carry burdens and regrets. And we all play a shell game of sorts, hoping to hide and deflect the broken places of our lives. But I say it's time to embrace truth.

So why not:

✳ Embrace the fact that you are a mess of magnificent proportions?
✳ Embrace the fact that you are not alone?
✳ And embrace the lavish reality of divine grace of such grand proportions? A divine grace that heals, restores, covers, forgives, renews, and abounds toward us as women!

What true freedom!

* 5 *

TALES FROM THE CRYPT

My official research for this chapter inadvertently began while shopping at the Michigan Avenue Nordstrom on the Magnificent Mile in downtown Chicago. It was the summer of 2001, and I was at my on-again-off-again-it's-an-odd-number-year, weight-loss low. *(Translation: I'd lost the twenty pounds gained the previous winter and could bend over and tie my shoes without oxygen supplement.)*

Hitting the "70 percent off the original price with an additional 15 percent on certain items" rack, I began piling out-of-season coordinates over my arm and made my way to the Crypt, aka the Pit of Despair. In other words, I entered *(dramatic drumroll, please . . .)* the Ladies' Fitting Room.

Can any good thing come from dressing rooms? Seriously, just think about it. And count all the dressing rooms you've stripped near naked in over the course of your lifetime. Are you any better for the experience?

My earliest recollection of a fitting room is of the one at Stephen's Toggery, a children's dress shop in Moberly, Missouri. I can't remember the name of the sisters who owned and managed it, but I'll never forget their hairstyles. It was the early seventies, and both their heads were piled high with elaborate twists and turns. Dozens of bobby pins, as well as the sprayed-on shellac of Aqua Net, kept each three-foot-high creation securely in place. It was there, at Stephen's, that an overzealous saleslady drew back a curtained partition and saw me in my five-year-old Skivvies. I nearly passed out from the embarrassment.

I have issues to this day—just ask my husband.

And then there was the dressing-room incident at Reichert's Department Store, owned by Mick and Jeannie Reichert, in my hometown of Brunswick, Missouri. It was a wonderful place. My best friend, Cindy Johnson (the niece of Mick), and I would stop there to check out the latest deliveries and shoe offerings each Saturday after eating a cheeseburger, fries, and dusty melon (a scoop of chocolate ice cream covered with marshmallow topping and sprinkled with malt flavoring) at the Uptown Cafe.

So it should come as no surprise that as a fifth-grader I was . . . well, a little on the short and squat side of adolescence. My mom and I were shopping for a new pair of pants, and it seemed I had tried on every one in the girl's section—to no avail. They just didn't fit. That's when Beulah Thomas suggested we might be able to find something on the *(brace yourself, girls, this is going to get ugly)* "Husky Boys" rack.

Gads! Talk about your female self-esteem killers. Sure enough, dear old mom spied a pair of wide-gauge corduroys and handed them to me through the sliver of door that I allowed her to open. Up and over the hips they went. Buttoned and zipped. Then I made the long, slow walk toward the trifold mirror. It was while walking that I first heard it.

Scritch, scritch, scritch.

What on earth was that? I continued three or four steps . . .
and heard it again.

Scritch, scritch, scritch.

Gazing downward as I took my last step or two, it suddenly
dawned on me: That horrendous annoying sound was the
sound of my thighs rubbing together in wide-gauge harmony!
Aurg! Someone just put me out of my misery! I stood there—
before my corduroy reflection—never comprehending the years
of fitting room horrors that lay ahead for me.

Nothing can zap the grace out of us faster than viewing our
bodies in ill-fitting garments. Nothing. And now as I closed the
Nordstrom door behind me, double-checked that it was locked,
and inspected the room for any hidden cameras, I began to listen
to the conversations and comments of the ladies around me. And
trust me, I wasn't eavesdropping. Those ladies were proclaiming
this stuff loud and clear. They didn't care who heard.

> Door #1: "I am such a cow."
> Door #2: "Oooo! I hate my thighs."
> Door #3: "This outfit isn't bad. But don't my ankles look fat?"
> Door #4: To her companion, "Do I look stupid in this?"
> Door #5: To her sister standing outside the door, "If I didn't
> have to *roll* my boobs up into my bra, this dress just might
> work." *(That one had the entire room hootin'!)*

Over and over women belittled themselves, demeaned their
bodies, and then requested sales staff to get them a few more
items so they could do it some more. Time and time again, I

marched before a trifold mirror and grunted with disgust at the sight before me.

Why do we do this to ourselves as women? Do men have three-way mirrors in their fitting rooms?

Here's what I think. People can only view you from one direction at one time. They're either getting a look at you from the front, one of your sides, or the back end. So, I say, forget the three-way mirror image! Forget the "rules" and the "laws" of fashion that keep you bound and go for the grace, baby.[8] You can start listening to the whispers and shouts of grace and discover how to live openly in divine freedom. And before the trifold mirror is as good a place to start as anywhere: Choose which side you want to look smashing from and work with that.

As for me, I try to look at my backside as little as possible. I never see it anyway, so why bother agonizing over it?

Now that's truth—outrageous, scandalous-grace truth!

✳ ✳ ✳

All of us need to be reminded of such truth now and again, for I find it so easy to live life in a small fashion—in "Smallville":

✳ Smallville: thinking that I am the pivot of everyone's life
✳ Smallville: allowing the wounds of my past to affect my present and future
✳ Smallville: discounting my talents, my gifts, my aspirations as "less than . . ."
✳ Smallville: tearing myself down with my own words and self-defeating thoughts

It wasn't until the summer of 1992 that I first hopped a train out of Smallville.

Do you remember the first adult girlfriend who told you a not-so-lovely truth—about yourself? We all have friends we can joke with and kick around complaints with, but what about that one friend who challenged you with something she said, or with a timely observation?

In the early nineties, I lived in Effingham, Illinois, with my husband and two children under the age of two. The majority of my days consisted of potty training (mostly cleaning up messes), mixing baby formula, and analyzing just how much weight I had gained since the week before. My one day of reprieve was on Sunday, when I got to drop off the kids at Sunday school and attend a "married couples" class with twenty other men and women. Adults who didn't spit up or cling to me like Velcro.

Ah, Sanity Central for fifty blissful minutes.

It was here, in this adult class, that my husband, Rick, and I met three couples who would become our closest friends: Bill and Becky Heiens, Rodney and Diana Hirtzel, and Rich and Lisa Hirtzel.

The female counterpart of each couple came to be my first official *adult* girlfriends. Each had passed the test. They'd laughed so hard at something I said that they snorted and routinely commented, "Oh, Julie, you are so funny!" *(Yes, my friendship criteria can be quite shallow.)*

Anyway, for close to three years, we spent nearly every Sunday afternoon or evening at one another's home. Impromptu lunches and hurried gatherings were par for the course, as well as shopping trips to St. Louis. I loved these women. They were a lifeline—no, make that a *sanity* line—for me as a young wife and mother. And they understood me.

Now on one particular day (not a Sunday) it had just been *one of those days.* My kids were driving me nutty. I felt fat and useless. And I had just read the latest issue of *Allure* magazine and realized I was never going to look like Cindy Crawford—no matter how much Revlon makeup I purchased. So, upon my husband's return from work that evening, I called up the girls and asked them to meet me for a therapy session. This consisted of a one- to two-hour meeting with food items such as Hostess Ho Hos, Ruffles potato chips, Prairie Farms French onion dip, and vast quantities of caffeine-laden beverages. We agreed upon the place and time, and met.

For the next hour or so I "shared" with my friends all my travails.

I told them the tops of my thighs were beginning to touch and how awful I was going to look in a swimsuit that summer. I showed them a white hair that I'd discovered sticking out from behind my ear just that morning, and then asked them if they could detect it from two—three—and then four feet away.

I voiced my concerns about the fine lines creeping around my eyes when they were squeezed shut. And I confessed to them that I felt like I no longer had it. "It" being the power of attraction with the male species in general. Oh sure, some guy had taken a second look at me only a few days before at Martin's grocery store, but my sense of female allure quickly dissipated as I caught a glimpse of my own backside and realized it was covered with a smattering of fuchsia Play-Doh.

Nope, not exactly *Sports Illustrated* Cindy Crawford material.

On and on I went until finally Becky put her hand on top of mine and said, "Julie, I want to show you something."

She proceeded to drag a set of salt and pepper shakers across the table where we were sitting. She picked up the salt and plopped it back down with a firm clunk. "This," she said, "is you." Then, as she picked up the pepper and slowly circled the salt, she said with a twinkle in her eye, "This is not the world." Resting both of her hands on mine, she looked me squarely in the eye and spoke girlfriend truth: "Julie, everyone isn't looking when you come into a room."

There was a silence in the heavens and the earth *(with the exception of Diana and Lisa murmuring a hearty amen)*.

Now let me ask you, how many of you reading this assume that I thought people were looking at me and thinking, *Why, that woman is absolutely stunning*?

That's what I thought you'd say.

See, I told you in the opening chapter that I thought we could become friends! You understand me, don't you? You really understand. For just like you, I seldom, if ever, assume that others are looking and admiring me. Rather, I'm inclined to believe that every eye is critiquing my clothes, my figure, my personality, and my demeanor. In my immature perspective I'd just assumed that, for good or for bad, all eyes were on me at church, while shopping, and everywhere else I might plant my foot.

The concept that I was actually going unnoticed in the world was absolutely liberating to me. For if this was true, it was not only within the realm of possibility, but all together likely, that no one noticed my up-and-down weight gains. It was possible that no one noticed my mismatched socks of navy and black.

And possible that the width of my rear end *(with the exception of its being highlighted with fuchsia Play-Doh polka dots)* was largely ignored by the grocery-store masses.

Becky's insightful observation offered a glimpse of girlfriend grace and expanded the shrinking worldview by which I had been living my life.

And I'm so glad she did. Her feedback has truly liberated me. Do I love dressing rooms now? Nope. I still call 'em "the Crypt" and sometimes wince at myself in the mirror. But I know now that the world no longer revolves around me.

Perhaps the next time you find yourself in the Crypt, you'll think of my friend Becky and the truth about three-way mirrors, and you'll graciously extend to yourself this liberating grace. And remember, never look behind you!

* 6 *

MAGIC PANTS

I'll never forget the clothes I was wearing as a student in Mrs. Herring's third-grade classroom or the evil spawn seated in the one desk in front of me. His name was Kip. Kip Railsback—aka *Damien.*

Who knows? Maybe at the time he was dealing with his own issues concerning his rust-colored hair and a freckled face. But for one reason or another, he was hell-bent on making year nine of my existence pure torture. His modus operandi? Heckling, name-calling, and verbal put-downs.

This particular day had started off on a bad note to begin with. A few weeks earlier I had received my first pair of non-rubber, non-ugly boots. In fact, I had begged for a pair until my mother finally gave up saying no and took me to Don's Bootery in Moberly, Missouri. There I was lined up with the coolest, multihooked, leather granny lace-up boots you've ever seen.

But Mom couldn't leave granny boots well enough alone. She insisted we go one step further and find the perfect outfit to go with said footwear. So we traveled to Kansas City and shopped at the downtown Macy's. Now I don't remember having anything specific in mind as a nine-year-old shopper. If memory serves correctly, I was more excited about the prospect of eating somewhere fancy than purchasing new clothing items. Nope, I didn't have anything in mind—but I certainly knew what I *didn't* want.

And that would be the "adorable" knickers ensemble that Mom brought back to the Girls' Dressing Room. *(Oh, the horrors of dressing rooms! But we've already covered that in "Tales from the Crypt"!)*

Knickers ensemble? Do you even remember what knickers are? And I'm not referring to the English version of underwear, either! I'm talking about the horrendous item of clothing that is, in effect, a pair of pants that got cut off at the knees! Has there ever been a time in modern history (with the possible exception of golfing wear) when knickers *were* in vogue? Or attractive to wear, for that fact?

I think not. And I wasn't buying it as a nine-year-old consumer in 1974, either. But Mom insisted I try them on, along with a coordinating shirt and vest.

You wanna take a guess as to what color this ensemble was?

Beige and rust.

Yep, beige, as in chapter 2, my "I hate the color beige" confession. And rust—the Color of the Beast.

This may be a good time to tell you a little bit more about my physical build as a third-grade girl and adult woman. I have been the chagrined possessor of "The Poodge" *(meaning the pocket of abdomen just below the belly button that refuses to lie down, mind its own business, and go away)* for more years than I care to think about.

Since the beginning of time (circa 1974) it has been the bane of my existence. For years I have tried low-fat diets, stomach crunches, pills, and even considered stomach tucking *(too painful, too expensive)* to remove The Poodge from my lower midsection. All to no avail. It's still there.

And it was there in the dressing room with me in 1974. Which made the following all the more intolerable.

The waistbands of both the knickers and the vest were made up of a wide band of stretch material. Galvanized rubber, I believe. The dueling *Kip rust* and *gourd yellow* stripes encircling the vest waistband was constructed of such a dense, stretchy, and insanely woven knit that Patriot missiles could have easily been launched from its base. Both waistbands were tight, clingy, and dreadful; they clung to my stomach like a bad habit.

For whatever as of yet undiagnosed self-esteem problems, as a nine-year-old I was already supersensitive to this part of my anatomy. So the last thing I wanted to do was draw attention to it. For I knew that it wouldn't be long before the redheaded Evil One—the one who had already poked fun at the size and color of my eyes *("camel eyes," he called them—see, I still remember, even after all these years)*, my olive complexion, and my loud laughter—would hone in on The Poodge. And as I gazed into the dressing-room mirror and saw myself in those horrid knickers and vest, just the thought of him making fun of my stomach made me want to throw up.

Cracking the door just so, as to ensure no one would view said horrendous outfit, I told Mom, "I don't like them."

"Oh, Julie, come out here and let me look at you. I'm sure you look absolutely adorable!" she replied.

Uh-huh, right. There was *no* way I was about to leave the safe confines of said room.

Sticking my head out farther, I tried again. "*Mooooom!* The pants are ugly and stupid looking, and I hate the colors beige and rust."

She didn't quite get it. "Well, they're called *knickers,* Julie, and they are a gorgeous crème and burnt sienna, sweetheart."

Crème and burnt sienna, eh? Well, they were still ugly. Even though I reiterated my profound dislike for the ensemble, when all was said and done, Mom won out *(not unlike the macaroni incident with my second-born child years later).*

We purchased the three pieces and made our way home with me in despair, sitting glumly in the passenger seat.

✳ ✳ ✳

That following Monday Mom suggested that I wear my new outfit. I declined. We did this for about a month until finally, on a November morning, she *insisted* that I wear it to school. So I pulled on those awful knickers and noted again their stretchy waistband. Pulling my arms through the striped shirt, I hit upon a brilliant plan. I would simply wear the vest over my *untucked* blouse. No waistband, no Poodge, and no Damien making fun of me. My plan lasted until I came out of my room and Mom and Dad both insisted that I "tuck in your shirt so everyone can see your cute outfit."

Being a rather compliant child, I obeyed without a word, but deep inside I simply wanted to die. If I had possessed a book bag at the time, I would have carried it in front of me during the entire day and hidden my shame *(as I've strategically done with various purses, jackets, and bridesmaid bouquets over the years).*

I will never forget that day.

Boarding the bus with my coat buttoned up like Fort Knox.

Trying to wear that coat to class—putting it away in my locker only after Mrs. Herring told me to do so.

Making a mad dash for my desk and sinking down into my chair.

Hoping desperately that the Almighty had struck Kip down with some cataclysmic illness that would render him unable to attend class.

And what strikes me most poignantly—even all these years later—is that I still remember looking down while seated in that chair. I remember noticing The Poodge that those awful knickers and vest seemed to make bigger and bigger with every second. And I remember crying, and feeling fat and ugly.

I left my desk twice that day, once to go to lunch and the other to gather my things for home and get in the bus-rider line. Walking with my arms bent "just so" *(any reader with stomach issues will know* exactly *what I'm talking about),* I collected my U. S. Presidents memorization homework and prepared to go to my locker.

I almost made it.

Seconds before the second bell was to ring, Kip spun his head and spewed: "Your stomach looks like a big fat pumpkin in those dorky pants."

Riiiiiiiiiiiiiiiiiiiiing.

I don't remember saying anything back to him because I thought he was right. I *did* look like a big fat pumpkin in those knickers. I hated them, and I knew every time I wore them, he would say something. So I vowed to never, ever, ever, ever, *ever* wear them again.

After collecting my coat and a few other things from my school locker, I stepped onto Rolla Henningson's bus and walked as far back as unspoken bus protocol would allow a third-grader to go. With my knee-length winter coat firmly clasped around my body, I proceeded to pull off those beige-rust knickers. Knotting them up into a tight ball beside me, I double-checked that my now bare legs—including my third-grade extremities of knees and upper thighs—were safely covered. Then joyously I stood, walked past six green uphol-stered bus seats, and shoved those knickers into a trash can placed in front of the back exit door! With each glorious shove—pushing them deeper and deeper beneath discarded paperwork, pop cans, and Kleenex tissues, I began to feel more and more free.

A quarter of a mile down the road, I stepped off the bus with Angie Woolston and waved good-bye to those knickers forever. I didn't have a clue what I was going to tell Mom and Dad when I got home. How exactly does one explain losing a pair of knick-ers *that one is wearing?*

But you know what? I didn't care. I didn't care how much trouble I got into. I didn't care if I was grounded. I didn't even care if I made my mom cry. I was free from the worry of pants that made my stomach look big—and that's all that mattered to me.

Now here's the truth. For nearly thirty years my top priority when clothes shopping, putting together an outfit, or appearing before a live audience of men and women, has been: *Hide The Poodge.*

The shape of my stomach, real or perceived, has been a

contentious fact of my life for nearly thirty years. No amount of reading books on loving my body *(oh, please!),* no amount of chanting positive self-talk, no amount of trying to compensate for this perceived fault with makeup or talent, has truly helped me shake my hang-ups regarding it.

And I'll go one step further in the truth telling. I can sooner accept grace and forgiveness in regards to sins and failures than accept grace for this area of my body. Trust me—I have been around the block, over the bend, and around the world when it comes to extending grace toward myself in this area of my physical features.

So why is that?

Can I blame it on Kip? I don't think so. Granted, his words weren't exactly a rocket booster for the development of strong self-esteem, but I was agonizing over my rolls before he came along.

Can I blame it on my parents? No, not at all. There wasn't one time that either of them commented on my weight or the size and shape of my figure.

How about the devil? Can I blame it on him? Well, I guess one could argue that the enemy of our soul loves nothing more than destroying the glorious reality of our creation. But honestly, I don't think it's even that.

I believe that my struggle (and yours too, perhaps) with accepting my body at such a young age—a struggle that continues somewhat to this day—rests in the fact that I am human and I am female. For whatever reasons, I seem predisposed to hone in on this part of my body as others of you are prone to do with various body parts and images. The size of our breasts, the shape of our noses, the projection of our ears, the length of our toes, the mass of our thighs, or any 1,000,001 other issues— most of us have at least one body area that we loathe and beat ourselves up about.

One area that we simply cannot imagine grace reaching.

Ah, but let's never underestimate the power of divine grace, or the fashionable ways in which it covers us. Now fast-forward to Dallas, Texas, 2002. I was on a ten-day business trip but managed to fit in some quality girlfriend time with Gracie and Cynthia, two Texas belles. In my book, quality time always encompasses some form of shopping and that's exactly where we found ourselves on a gloriously warm November morning. Malls the size of my Illinois community dotted the landscape, and both Gracie and Cynthia assured me that if I couldn't find what I was looking for in Texas, well, girlfriend, it simply couldn't be found.

We made our way in and around department stores with no luck. My faith was waning. Then Cynthia suggested that we go to a place called Chico's. "Julie, they have a marvelous line of clothes called the Travelers Collection, and you can practically sleep in them and they don't wrinkle." And since she and Gracie are both well aware of my aversion to beige, she added, "And they have gorgeous colors too!"

So I walked into Chico's, unaware of the audacious grace that was about to change my life.

Quickly enough, sales staff perused a dressing room and

collected an assortment of pants, blouses, and jackets for me to try on. Cynthia kept going on and on about the wearability and travel benefits of said items. Gracie commented on the beautiful jewel tones of said items. I noted the sizing on the tags—1, 2, or 3. Hey, I didn't care what they looked like! I was wearing a size 2 or 3 for the first time in my life—I loved this place!

Undressing quickly, I picked up a black pair of Travelers Collection pants. They slipped over my legs and thighs and fit comfortably around my waist. I pulled a matching sleeveless Travelers Collection tank over my head and finished it off with a ruby red jacket. There wasn't a mirror in the dressing room so I gingerly stepped out, hoping to catch a peek of myself without anyone noticing. No such luck.

I heard Gracie gasp. *Oh no,* I thought, heart sinking, *it's worse than I imagined.* Then I looked at my reflection and gasped. It took a moment for it all to compute, but as I stood before the dreaded three-way mirror, I realized this one incredible fact: I couldn't see The Poodge in those pants.

I turned this way and that way. I squinted my eyes and stared so hard my eyes about popped out. I even patted myself down like Stomach Girl in the Atlanta airport! *(Now you truly under-stand my reaction to that event!)*

Staring at myself, I then proclaimed to Gracie, Cynthia, and anyone else within a hundred-mile radius, "These are Magic Pants!"

Indeed, after a few decades of battling The Poodge, I could at last declare victory. I had finally found The Answer—and I didn't have to pay a plastic surgeon or buy any more books about loving my body *(thank goodness!).* It was as simple as discovering Magic Pants—otherwise referred to as "No Tummy" pants in Chico circles.

And then, just as I thought I would pass out from my grace-filled discovery, the sales staff suggested I finish off the look with a complementary belt. Say what? I hadn't worn a belt for years. Women with The Poodge seldom, if ever, place a band of leather around their waist. I was convinced this was the worst idea ever made by sales staff-kind.

Cynthia disagreed. "Julie, this belt would pick up the design in your jacket—now try it." *(Did I mention that Cynthia is wonderfully bossy?)* So just like that nine-year-old who tucked her shirt in on command, I allowed the sales lady to place the adjustable belt around my middle.

I just knew it was going to look awful. In fact, I wouldn't even look. I believe I heard Gracie's eyes rolling to the top of her head as she dutifully commanded, "Oh, open your eyes and take a look."

So I did. And you know what? It didn't look awful. In fact, it looked pretty marvelous! Ladies, for the first time in about ten years of adult life, I . . . had . . . a . . . discernable waistline!

Magic Pants created a "canvas" on which was placed a waist. Hallelujah!

Now, you may think I'm crazy, but I truly believe that this is a perfect example of outrageous grace in my life. God knows—*and I do mean, God himself knows*—how I have beat myself up over this issue in my life. He knows.

He knows that on certain days I have based my entire personhood on the shape of The Poodge. And as ridiculous or shallow as that may read to some of you *(or perhaps some of you know* exactly *what I mean)*—it is truth in my life.

But then, seemingly out of nowhere, God allowed me to find a miraculous pair of pants that could allow me to take my mind off The Poodge and think about other weighty matters. Instead of literal "weighty" matters!

I believe Magic Pants summarize the heart of God for women like me.

God knows our insecurities. He alone knows why we carry them around like a bag of bricks. Even though he has offered us abundant provision of grace (see Romans 5:17), he knows there are some things in life we just haven't been able to pray our way out of or "believe" our way past. He knows. And he continues to love us just as we are. And sometimes he allows us to discover one simple thing that can soothe a lifetime of pain.*

---

*Author reserves the right to forgo Magic Pants and seek professional help if deemed necessary.

7

Embrace Your Cellulite!

Part of this journey in discovering the exquisite joy of scandalous grace involves our coming to grips with certain realities of life. Not too long ago, I had an opportunity to do just that.

Lucky me.

It had quite possibly been the most incredible day of my speaking life. Interviewing with one of the most respected names in family radio, I had laughed and talked my way through a blissful meeting with Dr. James Dobson and cohost, John Fuller, at Focus on the Family in Colorado Springs, Colorado. Our scheduled half-hour taping had turned into an hour as we lost ourselves in conversation regarding the subject of motherhood and anger.

The day could not have gone better. I had remembered my hosts' names and hadn't said anything stupid. *(Which isn't an entirely unlikely possibility, if you must know.)* My hair had cooperated and was sticking up and out in the Halle Berry messy style I have come to embrace. And I was wearing a snazzy silk blouse accented by a kicky jacket from the miracle store: Chico's.

As I said my good-byes and drove back to my hotel,

I mentally patted myself on the back and thought, *Perfect, Jules, absolutely perfect.*

After parking my car, I made my way to my room. Sliding the key across the door latch, I stepped in and proceeded to get comfortable. Off came the dress slacks, silk blouse, and jacket. Off came the bra. *(Perhaps that was "T. M. I."—Too Much Information?)* Then I slipped into my flannel pajama bottoms and pulled my trusty Beach Blanket Babylon T-shirt over my head, ready to call it a day. But before ordering room service, I decided to wash up.

Stepping into the bathroom, I dampened a facial washcloth and begin to remove the day's makeup. Out of the corner of my eye, something garnered my attention. There was a fuzzy some-thing on the right side of my face—near my chin. Splashing warm water to clear the soapy mixture, I leaned toward the huge expanse of mirror. Closer still. Closer, closer, until . . . gasp!

I saw it.

Sprouting proudly from my face was a chin hair! Oh, it had tried to disguise itself, floating about with a wispy air of indifference, but it was clearly viewable under the glaring bathroom lights. I proceeded to pinch it between my fingers and began to pull. And pull. And pull. Good grief, that baby was well over forty feet long! *(Okay, maybe I'm overstating that just a bit, but it was a doozie.)*

And then it hit me.

That chin hair had been, in all likelihood, waving hello to the entire radio staff throughout our meeting. Forget my appearing on *Focus on the Family.* I had just performed on Focus on the Freaky Chin Hair!

Now that, my friend, just ain't natural or right, in my humble opinion. Just what is the deal with growing older and growing hair? It begins to reproduce itself in places it ought not. Like one's stomach, for instance. *(Not that I have any personal knowledge of this, mind you.)* And what about a woman's legs after age thirty or so? Do you find yourself slathering up for the ankle-to-thigh shave twice as often as you used to?

And speaking of shaving, what's with the underarm hair after a certain age? Last summer I was preparing for my appearance at the local pool when I noticed an underarm hair some four inches below home base. There it . . . sat? stood? grew? All by itself, just as proud as it could be. But where on earth had it come from? I called my best friend, Audrey, and asked her. She suggested that it may have been on my back—prior to the reduction surgery in '91. Well, that was a marvelous image to mull over!

Think of all the methods we women use and the money we spend to remove hair from our bodies.

We tweeze, wax, shave, use epilators, apply gels, purchase razor blades, sit quietly beneath laser beams, and apply depilatories *(*not *to be confused with suppositories).*

And I ask you, will this follicle battle ever end? No, I tell you. It will never end. Nor will a multitude of battles being waged on other fronts.

* * *

Last summer I spent a lot of time outside gardening (and lying by a pool) and got very dark. Now let me just say this. For those of you who are olive-complexioned or of Mediterranean descent, you'll understand the forthcoming statement completely. Being a great tanner is a two-edged sword of blessing. On the one hand, our skin toasts to an enviable shade and allows us to enjoy outdoor activities and water sports. On the other hand, we of great tanning descent tend to be "hairy."

Yep, hairy—as in chin hairs sprouting and hairdressers asking, "Do you mind if I shave your neck?"

So there you go.

Now as I was saying, this particular summer found me browner than I had been in years. I was teaching an adult women's class on Sunday morning and had just made my way into the room when my good friend Margie walked in, sat down, looked at me, and said, "Oh, you are so dark. I hate you."

Because she's a good friend (and it was a church class, after all) I made an allowance for her vehement statement and did not kick her out. Instead, I gazed at her unbelievably smooth, porcelain complexion and spoke profound truth. "Margie, my friend, embrace your whiteness!"

Have you ever heard such wisdom? Okay, you have, but as a result of that encounter, "Embrace your . . ." became my mantra for life. Because honestly, there are a lot of realities that I've found difficult to deal with over the years. Some funny. Some not. Some I can more easily forget. Others seem to play over and over in my mind like a bad movie clip.

The toughest things for me to embrace—to accept and let go—have had to do with the aging process of life. I mean, it's simply ridiculous how your mind and body (and even your own kids!) gang up against you after age thirty.

Take my son Patrick, as an example. One day—he was about three years old at the time—I was lounging in the family-room recliner, just minding my own business, when he toddled into the room and asked me to "love on him." What mother can resist that? *(Trust me, I should have!)* So I picked him up, snuggled him close to my side, and kissed the top of his head. I'm sure I threw in an "I love you more than anything!"–type statement too.

So there we were. Me loving on my son. Patrick thinking.

A moment or so later he tried to wiggle his little hand into my pants pocket. Then he grinned impishly and asked, "Whass that, Momma?"

I had no idea what he was talking about, so I said kindly, "Patrick, I don't have anything in my pocket."

He wasn't buying it. Again he prodded in my pocket and, this time, squealed with delight. "Whass that in your pocket, Momma, whass that?!"

This kid wasn't going to quit! So I reached into my pocket . . . and began to feel light-headed. A thin glaze of sweat popped out on my forehead. "Whass that" was my stomach! Resting on my lap, as God intended it to!

But that wasn't the end of the queries. Oh no. Patrick seemed to be particularly gifted in that area of research.

A couple of years later, after observing me walk away from him across the kitchen floor, he asked, "Mommy, why do you do this"—jiggling his hands—"when you walk?"

I surrender! I'm waving the white flag, and I'm laying down my arms. As well as my stomach, thighs, and chin hairs. I have now come to embrace the mantra I first told Margie that summer morning.

Embrace your cellulite.
Embrace your stretch marks.

Embrace your chin hairs. *(Pluck them, for goodness' sake, but mentally embrace them.)*
Embrace the thin, crepe *(not creepy)* lines that are forming around the corners of your eyes.
Embrace your memory loss.
Embrace your memory loss. *(Did you catch that repetition? If so, you have nothing to worry about!)*
Embrace the miracle of underwire.

Really, I'm telling you, this can be absolutely liberating theology to live by!

Embrace your inability to sing and clap on rhythm.
Embrace your Poodge with a side of Magic Pants.
Embrace your poor math skills. *(After all, five-fourths of American women have trouble with fractions.)*
Embrace the popping sound coming from your kneecaps.
Embrace your off-key singing voice.
Embrace the fact that you are indeed, a lot like your mother, and it's not all a bad thing.
Embrace the medicinal cure of chocolate. *(It always makes me feel better.)*
Embrace the fact that you do not have it all together.
Embrace your past—good, bad, and forgotten.
Embrace your present—right here, right now.
And embrace your future—knowing that scandalous grace will accompany you, making you strong in the grace that is in Christ Jesus all along the way.[9]

* 8 *

THE INCREDIBLE SHRINKING WOMAN

Ugly knickers weren't the only unwanted items I came to possess in third grade.

In the spring of that year, I began to notice swelling on my previously flat chest. I was convinced something was wrong with me. After all, it would be another two years before I found myself sequestered with twelve other giggling fifth-grade girls in a darkened classroom, listening to the embarrassing 8 mm film–footage of *Your Body and You.*

I hadn't a clue what those bumps were doing on my chest. Maybe I was allergic to something? I had a friend who once ate peanut butter and then blew up like a puffer fish. Perhaps that was it. Or maybe I had bruised myself somehow—causing odd swelling on both sides of my chest. Or maybe . . .

Okay, so I wasn't the brightest crayon in the box. It wasn't until my mother commented and literally spelled it out for me— "Why, Julie, you are starting to get your b-r-e-a-s-t-s"—that I came to understand. *(Give me a hanky wave if your mother routinely s-p-e-l-l-e-d or whispered words.)*

Well, that's just what I needed. As if The Poodge wasn't

enough to worry about, now I had another mutinous part of my body ganging up on me. As it turned out, not only was I the lone third-grade girl wearing a bra to school in my class, I was the only nine-year-old whose mother insisted on her being properly fitted for one. *(Do you hear familiar strains of the Crypt beginning to creep in?)*

I remember Patterson's Department Store in Moberly, Missouri, to this day. Walking past menswear and jewelry, my mother and I made our way up the back stairway, turned slightly to our left, and landed smack in the middle of the strangest place I had ever been. Hanging from display racks were molded bra cups the size of cereal bowls. I looked down and concluded that I hadn't eaten nearly enough Wheaties. A sea of lace, underwire, and "foundational garments" surrounded me as Mom stood by the help counter. We seemed to wait forever. And just as I began to hope we'd leave, a middle-aged woman appeared and my mother asked, "Is there anyone here who can help fit my daughter with her first bra?"

Say what?

Please tell me that did not mean what I think it means, I begged inwardly.

And who, exactly, was *anyone?* Surely not the salesclerk speaking to my mother or the dowager folding underwear in the Slip and Satin section of lingerie.

But sure enough, quicker than you can say "cross your heart," I was in a dressing room. Now you may wonder, *Julie, is there anything worse than being fitted for a bra?* Um, yes. Being fitted for one at age nine! My memory gets a bit cloudy at this point, but I distinctly recall the dowager ordering me to bend forward slightly to get "the girls" *(yep, that's what she called them!)* into proper position. I was rendered speechless and mortified. It was ghastly. But as we left I could rest assured that I was filling the proper cup *(negative AAA, I believe).*

I went back to school the next day, and the oddest thing happened. Boys—fifth-grade boys, even—who only the day before had never noticed me now felt compelled to snap my bra strap while walking by. Others snickered, pointed, and commented about my different shape. Even my best boy-pal, who shall remain nameless, acted goofy. Good grief, what was up with all that?

Ever since, "the girls" and I have been engaged in a love-hate relationship. We've had our ups (teens to early thirties) and our downs (post breast-feeding). And it isn't in any small part due to the fact that ever since I showed up with "the girls," the male species began to act, well, how do I say this? . . . stupid.

For the life of me, I could not figure out what the big deal was about my having breasts. *(Actually, the term* nubs *would have been more appropriate.)* How could two puffy places on the chest cavity of life cause those with XY chromosomes to act so odd?

It wasn't just boys' attitudes that changed. As the year passed, then two and three more, I continued to develop. And with the continued attention of the boys came a less-than-friendly attitude from my girlfriends—the nub-less ones. Suddenly I found myself on their enemy list. And what was my crime? Had I gossiped and talked mean about them? No. Did I throw a birthday party and not invite them? No. I had been tried and found guilty of the treasonous act of developing before they had.

It occurred to me, on more than one occasion, that *"the girls"* were going to be far more trouble than they were worth.

Now some of the male species might question my taking an entire chapter to discuss female mammary glands. They might understand pictures and drawings—but thoughtful discussion, well, I think not. But women understand the need completely.

Women understand that "feeling" like a woman and "looking" like a woman are profoundly tied to the development, size, and shape of the female bust. We know what it's like to feel inadequate and insufficient based upon our chest glands. And we know what it's like to have people form opinions and impressions based on what they do or do not see.

But I can only speak from my own experience and trust me, there was a lot to see! As I told you previously, I began to develop quite early. By the time I hit high school I could have more than filled the cereal bowls I first saw at Patterson's. And I wasn't particularly pleased with that fact, for it seemed to me that all my breasts did was get in my way.

I loved playing softball and basketball but found myself instead thinking more about the manner in which my chest was moving than if I was going to make it safe to home plate or down the court in time for a breakaway layup. It probably didn't help that a friend had commented during routine basketball practice, "Julie, you bounce higher than the basketball!" I know now she meant it in fun, but from that moment on I began to run slower ("less bouncy") with my arms crossed slightly against my chest.

I suppose there are plenty of busty teens and women who are comfortable with their size. But I was never one of them. I began to buy minimizer bras, wore loose flannel shirts nearly my entire senior year of high school, and stepped into the shower (mandatory gym class rule) with a towel wrapped around me in the locker room. I even quit playing sports.

I just didn't like standing out *(pardon the pun)*. And I was never comfortable with the attention I received from men because of it.

After high school I was hoping that attending a Christian college— one filled with Christian men, right? —would set me up for better experiences with those of the testosterone set. I was wrong. All too often while meeting and talking they too would drop their gaze eighteen inches or so from my eyes and just stare.

Sigh.

All I wanted was for someone of the male species to notice something *other* than the size of my bustline. I wanted to count for something more than an alphabetical letter size and have my thoughts, opinions, and personality stir up greater interest than "the girls."

Eventually I married and thought I could put all those feelings aside. At last I had a man who wanted to talk with me. A man who encouraged my dreams of writing and speaking. At last those concerns could be put to rest.

But then I had children. And after each pregnancy, while my stomach returned to its previous size, "the girls" continued to grow.

And grow.

And grow.

By age twenty-five, I was packing a "bosom" rather than

breasts, and I couldn't fit into an off-the-rack bra to save my life. My back began to hurt. Grooves began to form over my shoulders. And every person I met (male or female at this point) seemed to zero in on the bosom and the bosom only. I hated my shape and I hated the attention "the girls" continued to garner.

Now I need to add a marital disclaimer in the midst of this chapter. I married a man who appreciated all of me—my sense of humor, personality, my tendency to dream big but get lost in the details—and yes, he appreciated "the girls." Loved *and appreciated them. So that will make the following all the more poignant and help you appreciate my husband all the more.*

Rick knew how I felt about my breast size and he understood—*despite his reassurances that he loved my body and considered me "perfect"*—that I would never like the way I looked in or out of clothes. He listened to my frustrations and suggested that I see a plastic surgeon and discuss the option of breast-reduction surgery. And then he suggested that he could sell his stock options for the year to pay the deductible portion of the insurance.

Now is that a man willing to sacrifice for his woman or what?!

I did just that, and my surgeon, Dr. Hart, suggested that he meet with Rick also. He felt it important for the husband to express his feelings regarding such a dramatic change to his wife's appearance. So Rick did. Together we discussed the pros (able to see toes when looking down) and cons (scarring, possible loss of sensitivity) and together decided to schedule the procedure.

I went under the knife September 30, 1991, and wrote the following in my journal, under the influence of Demerol, a few hours post-op.

It's 7:55 P.M. and I had the surgery. Thank you, Jesus, for not letting me die. You know I didn't want my obituary to read: Death by Breast Reduction. I appreciate that. I ask for quick recovery so I can take care of Kristen and Ricky and more than anything I'm grateful that people will at last be able to notice Julie the Christian rather than Julie the Chest. Thanks for understanding how important this was to me.

I suppose some may consider my thinking and my surgical procedure rather shallow. After all, aren't we supposed to "accept ourselves just as God made us"? I guess that point could be made. However, this is what I found to be true in my life. Through this battle with "the girls," I discovered that God cared about every detail of my existence.

Over the years, I had written various prayers and petitioned the Almighty with a plethora of serious things. But it wasn't until I talked with God about my breasts—*yes, I know that sounds ridiculous*—and all my dissatisfaction, insecurities, and frustrations related to them, that I caught my first whiff of the aroma of divine grace. The kind of grace that, according to Hebrews 4:16, truly helps us in our time of need.

✳ ✳ ✳

So what's my story post-reduction? Well, I can finally wear a blouse with darts. I no longer have to buy jackets four sizes larger than my pants. And I haven't noticed anyone ogling my bust (except my husband) for more years than I can remember.

I guess the best thing post surgery is that no one notices me one way or the other. When I talk to men and women, eye contact is maintained without fail.

As I made my way through a crowded convention floor last July, I never thought about the projection of my bust or if anyone else was noticing it. I simply walked, like normal women do every day, and blended in with the rest of the men and women around me.

I no longer feel like I'm walking around with a label reading *Julie: Chesty Girl.* As a result of my "downsizing," I've been freed from that mental label I was convinced everyone else read.

Julie, the incredible shrinking woman, found *herself.* Sans gargantuan cup and twelve-hooked bras.

Now suppose I were to ask, "What label are you carrying around?" How would you respond? If you were given the opportunity to have a surgical strike against that label, what would you be freed to do? to believe? to feel? How many of those labels, do you suppose, are part of the construction of your heart and consciousness, anyway?

I believe we're all magnificent creations of multilayered needs, desires, passions, fears, hopes, emotions, heartaches, and joys, and yes, even self-imposed labels. I believe that each of us is constructed, if you will, by these varying layers and that each plays a significant role in the manner in which we both view and live our lives. But far too few of us have taken the time to examine these layers. Or perhaps we've not allowed ourselves the freedom to examine and question its place in our lives.

✳ ✳ ✳

Not that long ago I enjoyed a delectable apple dessert at a restaurant in Wheaton, Illinois. It consisted of a baked apple ensconced within simple phyllo pastry and floating on a luscious island of caramel sauce with a cool scoop of vanilla bean ice cream. I swooned as I took my first bite. The buttery puff pastry positively melted in my mouth, and I was intrigued by the multiple layers that made up the shell in which the apple was baked.

Using the tines of my fork, I began to separate, then count . . . one, two, three, four, five, six, seven, eight, nine, ten . . . on and on until I stopped at forty-four individual layers. Forty-four whisper-thin sheets of pastry made up one individual puff shell. I thought about this for a moment or two and then said to myself, "I'm a puff pastry girl." My life consists of varying layers that create and sometimes shroud the woman I truly am. But the puff pastry of life needs to be examined, considered, and counted in order to discover who we *really* are, at the core, behind all the layers.

When I tell women about my issues with "the girls," some laugh. And some cry. But all relate because we all have something in our life that we just can't seem to get over, around, or past. Things that, no matter what we tell ourselves we're "supposed" to believe or no matter how tired our girlfriends are of hearing about them, just never get resolved. Beth Moore, in her powerful teaching video *Breaking Free,* has this to say about those layers of need: "Jesus never grows tired of the length nor the depth of your need."[10]

And how right she is.

Think about it, ladies. For close to twenty-six years, I talked to God about the size of my breasts. Twenty-six years. Can you imagine listening to me talk that long about something so, well, fleshly? Can you imagine the Creator of the universe taking time to listen? It sounds crazy, that one so divine would consider one so earthly. But I can tell you with absolute certainty, God did. He listened. He cared. And he made a way for me to throw off the label that had boxed me in for so many years.

Much like Magic Pants, scandalous grace lavished me yet again with the audacious reality of the divine.

And oh, how I needed it.

And oh, how we all need it.

9

THE "OTHER" WOMAN

Her name was Mindy. And from the instant I saw her, I knew I would never be able to compete.

Her glossy mane tumbled down between her thin shoulder blades and framed her perfect nose, perfect teeth, perfect cheekbones, perfect eyebrows, perf—. Well, you get the perfect picture.

It was as if every sound that came out of her perfect mouth was one brilliantly scripted jewel after another. She was funny. Witty.

And thin. Boy, was she thin. In fact, it was the Gloria Vanderbilt jeans that she wore so well that became the final straw for me. After seeing her in said formfitting denim, with a swan embroidered in gold thread on the pocket, I went to a department store and bought a pair of my own, somehow hoping to garner the same attention she had.

Alas, my swan was but an ugly duckling.

My legs were too short, so I cuffed the hem once, then twice. The inseam crept in areas it ought not and, as a result, the golden-threaded swan that graced Mindy's protruding hipbones came to protrude from a portion of my body NOT connected to the hipbone.

That's when I decided to throw in the towel. So it was on a cool spring evening in April 1978 that Mindy McConnell (aka actress Pam Dawber of *Mork & Mindy* fame) became the first victor in my never-ending competition with the "other" woman.

Let's face it, ladies, we have all seen the enemy. And she makes us feel inferior. Can you recall the "other" woman in your life? You may have been quite young. Or in your early teens. But something about her just "went all over you," as my mother would say.

Maybe it was the color and texture of her hair.

Or the confident manner in which she spoke.

Perhaps you noticed her because she seemed to be everything you wished you could be.

Her clothes seemed to fit right.

The cute boys liked her.

She was able to attend college instead of working full time to help support a family.

The possibilities are endless, but the bottom line is this: You considered her better or prettier or smarter or more talented or just plain *luckier* than you. And those thoughts made you mad, probably jealous, and may have propelled you to either live your life as a competition against her or as one of quiet "poor me" resignation.

But how does that "other" woman affect your life?

Profoundly, as we'll see.

I admit I enjoy watching people. I'm constantly amazed at the diversity and complexity of the men and women that I see while grocery shopping, waiting at airport gates, or pulling up alongside a busy intersection. I enjoy watching people—not to make fun of them or judge them, but to simply witness the relational dynamics at work in individuals. And to watch the amazing kaleidoscope of emotions that each and every human displays.

I saw such a display at my local Hy-Vee grocery store three summers ago. My husband was shopping with me, and we were in aisle three, checking out tomato sauces. It was the middle of a July afternoon, and the temperatures were scorching. Even with a pair of shorts and a sleeveless tank top on, I was hot and uncomfortable.

So there we stood that summer day, thoughtfully considering the difference between Prego and Ragu. About three feet ahead of us was a woman in her late forties or early fifties. She looked a little frazzled. Her hair was a bit messy, and she seemed very self-conscious of the clothes she was wearing. Her clothes didn't look bad. In fact, they looked perfectly fine. But I noticed that she tugged at her shorts a bit and pulled her shirt out and over them as she made her way closer to Rick and me.

She just didn't look comfortable in her skin, if you know what I mean.

About that time another woman approached from the opposite side of the lane. She looked to be in her late thirties or early forties. Her legs were tanned, and they enhanced the jolt of berry red fabric that her shorts and shirt were made of. As she passed Rick and me, she smiled and said a quiet hello. She was pretty. And exuded an air of kindness.

I then watched as she drew closer to the woman who seemed uncomfortable in her skin. That frazzled-looking woman caught the eyes of the younger woman and then lowered her head. She became quite intrigued with the labeling instructions on a can of refried beans she was holding. Keeping her head down as the tanned woman passed, she then slowly turned and watched her exit out of the aisle.

I could tell that she was giving that girl a serious once-over.

She then turned back, caught my gaze, and rolled her eyes to the top of her head as if to say, "Would you get a load of her?"

Well. That interchange was most compelling.

The dynamic at work in that Hy-Vee food aisle was a perfect example of what women are doing every day, everywhere, from every age bracket. Sizing each other up—judging themselves based on the appearance of another. Comparing supposed weaknesses and trying to make themselves feel better by ignoring or brushing off one another.

What amazes me about all this is that we never have to be "taught" to do this as women. It just seems to come instinctively. No one has to hand us a primer and instruct us in the ways of comparison, envy, jealousy, inferiority, competition, and cattiness. Girls just seem to "know" how to do all those things.

Now trust me, I'm not a female female-basher. It isn't my intention to denigrate my comrades in estrogen or to make women sound like they never mature mentally past age six. Not at all. But I've come across a few diaries from my youth, as well as watched my own teenage daughter interact with her friends since preschool, and I am struck by the overall propensity of females to indulge in frustrating games of comparison.

I know that in my own life, I have never lacked for thinking about the "other" woman, whom I always assume is better than I. If she's not an actual, living, breathing creature, then she's an ideal I carry with me in my head. And oftentimes, the "other" woman has turned out to be someone I'm close to, such as an acquaintance from church, a woman at work, or even a relative. Yikes! Perhaps, for better or worse, the "other woman" is our own mom.

What's the problem with all this? Simply put, when we allow ourselves to buy into the concept of comparison, we limit our own ability to interact with women around us. When our thoughts are filled with worrying about those we perceive as better or "other" than we are, we are in fact limiting and changing the way we think about ourselves and how we relate to others. We are cutting off the very supply chain of female friendships that we were created to enjoy.

As usual, I have another story from the front to make my case.

Several years ago I was invited to the home of a new acquaintance. I had met Stacey at church and thought we might have a lot in common. She and her husband had eaten dinner with Rick and me. Over barbequed steak and baked potatoes, we women agreed that we should get together at her place sometime the next week.

About three days later I called to get directions to her house and was taken aback by the street address she gave. She had named a certain subdivision out by the car dealership. But surely she hadn't meant *that* subdivision. It was in *the* neighborhood.

You know what I'm talking about—every town has one. It's the neighborhood you tool through on negative-checkbook-balance weeks, just to make yourself feel a little more lousy. It's the neighborhood that makes you curse your lot in life (your house lot, that is) and makes you realize that you can't even afford the mulching attachment on the John Deere yard tractor being used to manicure the lawns.

Well, Stacey lived there. And finding out her address is all it took for that first inkling of "other woman" thinking to enter my thoughts. *Well, she couldn't possibly live out in that neighborhood,* I argued. *After all, she has to be four years younger than I. She and her husband couldn't possibly live there.*

So I packed up my two children at the time, Kristen and Ricky, and headed toward her house.

To be honest—and I'm almost always honest—I was really hoping that she lived on a peripheral street near the neighborhood. Maybe her house sat parallel to the street bordering the area. Somehow I was hoping Stacey hadn't made the cut. I was hoping she lived in a neighborhood . . . well, like mine. When I thought back to my living room, kitchen, and dining room, where I had served her and her husband dinner, I began to cringe. Suddenly Stacey wasn't simply another female and young mother. And our potential friendship was on the line—all because of address differences. The anxious feelings I had while driving across town, the insecurity that was beginning to creep in around the corners . . . well, they attested to the mental comparisons that I was throwing around in my mind.

I pulled to a stop on a spotless, concrete driveway, which made me very nervous because my car leaked oil. As she walked from the house and greeted the kids, my eyes were drawn to the gorgeous, professional landscaping around the perimeter of her lawn. Good grief! This woman had more money in perennials than I had in my savings account. One bag of mulch equaled two cans of powdered baby formula in my world.

The children followed Stacey inside. I slithered behind.

As I stepped into her living room, I heard myself gasp—out loud, at that. There, before my very eyes, was a room straight from an Ethan Allen showroom floor. The carpet was plush, the color of a white, sandy beach. *(Not that I had ever seen a white, sandy beach, but I bet Stacey had.)* Stylishly swagged across her windows were *not* cotton panels from the local Wal-Mart, but exquisitely beautiful, cranberry-hued draperies.

As she led us through that stunning room, casually chatting with the children, I began to feel sick to my stomach. With a faux smile plastered on my green face, I followed her through her well-appointed home.

I saw a refrigerator the size of a small toolshed.

A snack bar with chairs upholstered in white leather.

An enormous television screen that filled the family-room wall.

Finally, we made our way down to the "playroom"—or the basement, as those in my neighborhood commonly referred to this area of the house—which looked suspiciously like my living room. I believe it was at this point that I officially passed out.

You know what? I can't remember anything about that day—other than the twisting knife of comparison and envy that all but gutted my enjoyment. Stacey was a wonderful hostess; she made my children feel welcome. Her home exuded a warmth and comfort that I so prized for my own.

But I didn't hear a word Stacey may have said that day. Nor do I recall engaging her in any conversation that drew out information regarding her life—her heart—or any joys or pains she may have been experiencing.

That's because my covetous—and comparing—spirit was evaluating everything I saw in her home. From the porcelain figurines in a cherry curio cabinet to a five-piece furniture suite in her ample master bedroom, I just couldn't stop comparing her things to mine. The more I thought about it, the shorter my end of the stick seemed to be getting and the "less" I began to feel about me.

Sadly enough, Stacey probably had no idea that all of this comparison game was going on in my mind. Or perhaps she did sense a barrier go up, an air of self-sufficiency that came across as being aloof and rude.

I never did see Stacey after that visit.[11] And you don't have to be a rocket scientist to figure out why. I allowed my warped, distorted thoughts to short-circuit any possible friendship. That day, just because of where she lived and the type of home she had, I set up Stacey as the "other" woman. And I labeled her as the enemy rather than as a potential friend.

The *other* woman I couldn't possibly have anything in common with.

The *other* woman who was easier to stereotype than to get to know.

The *other* woman whose heart I valued less than my own feelings of inferiority.

So what was it exactly that caused me to interact with Stacey *(or more aptly, not interact)* in the manner I did? This question isn't too hard for me to answer. After all, I can now examine my life and see that *my own* perceptions about money (what it can and can't buy), as well as the physical specifics of looking attractive (being thin, having a flat stomach), have most greatly shaped my insecurities and "other" woman tendencies.

What about you? Is there an "other" woman lurking in your life?

Perhaps she was a model on an early 1980s cover of a teen magazine. I still recall photographs of Dara Sedaka, the daughter of music legend Neil Sedaka, in a *Teen* magazine spread in the early eighties. And from there, the comparisons began.

Dara was gorgeous, with her silky brown hair parted down the center of her head. But when I tried that hairstyle, my head resembled an upside-down tulip.

Dara had adorable freckles that enhanced her non-pimply cheeks. I had a brown mole above my top lip that a friend's little brother once called "a black booger."

Dara was perfect. I was a far cry from perfect.

So for years—more than I'm even willing to admit—I kept trying to live up to her image. And, of course, I failed miserably.

Maybe the "other" woman in your life was a once-only encounter. Maybe you don't even know her name. You simply saw her while driving to work or passed her on a busy street corner while shopping. But you noticed her. And found yourself comparing whatever against her.

Now here's the crazy thing. For all my insecurities and issues with a stomach that won't lie flat and surgical procedures to control sundry parts of my body, I've begun to realize that I have been the "other" woman in another woman's life. Is that crazy or what?

Do you recall my girlfriend Cynthia, who led me to the Promised Land of Magic Pants and Chico's? Well, let me give you a little more background about the two of us. I think you'll feel a whole lot better about your own struggles after hearing our tale.

* * *

I first met Cynthia Spell-Humbert in the crowded lobby of an Atlanta, Georgia, hotel. We were both attending the annual Christian Booksellers Association Convention and participating in a women's-only meeting of writers and speakers from across the country. It was 2001, and I was as green as green can be when it comes to events like this. In fact, I carried my camera around my neck, hoping to get a candid shot with someone like Billy Graham or Jan Karon. I reeked "newcomer."

Anyway, the women's event (the AWSA: Advanced Writer Speaker Association) had maintained an E-mail digest the previous twelve months. So even though most of us weren't able to recognize one another by physical features, we could quickly talk E-mail posts and figure out who was who. Cynthia had posted such a message a week or so earlier, stating that she would be arriving with her mother and baby girl. So when I saw a woman enter the foyer with a baby stroller, a baby, and a mother-looking figure behind her, well, call me a genius, but I assumed it was Cynthia.

I immediately walked over to her, threw my arms around her,

and asked, "Hey, are you the 'I'll be bringing my baby so pray for me' Cynthia from the digest?"

She was. We chatted for a brief time. I met her mother. Checked out the baby. And told her how much I admired her commitment to attend with her nursing baby. I didn't tell her that I had never gotten past the "it hurts so I'm quitting" stage of breast-feeding with any of my three babies. We probably spent a total of four minutes talking. Nothing profound was said. It was merely two complete strangers meeting for the first time.

I had already checked in, and it was time for Cynthia to secure her room with the hotel management. So I gave her a quick good-bye hug and made my way back to my room.

This is the inner dialogue I carried on with myself while waiting for the elevator to ding. . . .

Boy, is she ever gorgeous! And thin. I have never seen a woman's stomach so flat after having a baby. Good grief, my stomach hung out for months after Patrick was born. And her hair, did you get a look at that hair? That is the prettiest blonde color I have ever seen. I bet she wears Ann Taylor clothes—she just looks like an Ann Taylor woman. And how tall do you think she was? Five-foot-six or seven? Honestly, I felt like a rectangle there beside her. A short and stubby rectangle. I should have lost thirty pounds before coming down here to Atlanta. I should have at least brought my body shaper! She's thin, she's gorgeous, and I bet she has money too. She just looks like she does. Sigh. *I feel so fat. And I wonder how much credit I have on my Visa?*

I kid you not. I thought of *all* those shallow, sad thoughts on my way to the fifteenth floor. Now let me clarify something. I didn't "dislike" Cynthia at all. I simply found myself making those mental confessions of inferiority, insecurity, and comparison—that always, always, always signals my setting someone up as the "other" woman.

The day came and went, and I didn't see Cynthia again. The following afternoon I caught a glimpse of her wheeling her baby into the prayer lunch that I was attending. She looked even prettier than she had the day before. Humph!

Within a few moments our hostess welcomed us all and instructed us to enjoy our lunch. I did just that. Then she returned and told us that we would each be given four minutes to sum up our year and request any specific prayers from one another. About thirty women did this, including Cynthia, who, much to my surprise, shared with all of us her struggle with depression and as the last one closed, our host then asked us all to join together for corporate prayer.

I don't know about you, but I think one of the best sounds in the world is that of women's voices praying. I love to hear the varying cadence and inflection as each one verbalizes her love for God and for one another. And this moment was to be just that—an outpouring of voices requesting God's presence in their midst and in the lives of one another, and direction for their speaking and writing.

I was listening. And thankful, so thankful, for being a part of something bigger than myself or any one woman in that room. I was agreeing with the words being spoken when a thought came to me: *Go across the room, place a hand on Cynthia, and pray for her.*

So I did. Standing up, I looked around, saw her kneeling on the floor about ten feet away from me, and walked toward her.

I don't even think she knew I was there beside her as I knelt close to her, placed my hand on her left knee, and prayed silently.

I didn't know what to pray—but Cynthia's and my Divine Father did. My mind filled with words, asking for her to sense his love. I prayed for any wounded places that there might be deep within her soul. And I prayed that God would forgive me for assuming so many things about Cynthia . . . things that, in the light of eternity, just did not matter. About that time Cynthia grabbed my hand and squeezed it tightly. As soon as we were dismissed, she turned toward me, threw her arms around me, and hugged me like crazy.

And then I said the stupidest thing. I looked at her, smiled, and said, "I just want you to know something . . . Prozac is my friend."

Say what! Where on earth did that come from?

As soon as the words came out of my mouth I wanted to sweep them back in and throw them out. What kind of moronic statement was that? And who—but me—would even say it?

But something funny happened. As soon as Cynthia heard those words—processed those words—she began to cry and hugged me again. Only this time she hugged me even tighter. We began to laugh that emotionally unstable laugh that girl-friends do. Not really sure of what was so funny but caught up in the sheer pleasure of the sound.

And here's the truly humorous part of all this. This "other" woman—whom I had convinced myself was prettier, smarter, wealthier, and more talented—had, in fact, checked out *my* Web site just a few days previous to the conference. After reading through the material and viewing my photograph, Cynthia had herself decided that I was the "other" woman—the one who had it all together professionally and had oodles of extra income to fritter away on Web site graphics and postings.

So there I was—standing right beside her and telling her that Prozac was my friend.

Trust me: Women who have traversed the dark trail of depression hold a soft spot for fellow travelers. And that was just what we were—fellow journeywomen in life. For all our perceived beauty, talents, spunky personalities, and flat *(or otherwise)* stomachs, we were very much alike.

We had both carried the weight of depression. Both of us had experienced the excruciating pain of abandonment. And both had warred with presumptive thoughts regarding other women.

Had it not been for God's prompting, I never would have sought to know Cynthia. She intimidated me. And I would just as soon not hang out with women who make me feel that way.

But there's the rub: Cynthia didn't really "make" me feel any way. *I* chose to compare, *I* chose to presume, and *I* chose to limit my expectations of our interaction with each other.

This cycle of setting up another woman as the "other" woman affects our expectations about what we can and cannot do.

She has a college degree; I don't. Therefore we cannot have much in common.

She is married with children; I am single and loving it. Therefore our common interests would be limited, at best.

She doesn't believe in walking around the mall and just window-shopping; I always have a mental list of things to pick up. Therefore she's a financial tightwad and not for me.

Do you see what this cycle of limited expectations does—and how it can go on and on and on, if we let it? All of us have choices to make.

From kindergarten to the grave, we can lock ourselves into such thinking. We can demean our selves and live with the constant insecurity of not being as good as that "other" woman. We can limit our relationships.

Or we can embrace who we really are—the women God has made us uniquely to be. After all, as Psalm 139 says,

> Oh yes, you shaped me first inside, then out; you formed me in my mother's womb. I thank you, High God—you're breathtaking! Body and soul, I am marvelously made! I worship in adoration—what a creation! You know me inside and out, you know every bone in my body; You know exactly how I was made, bit by bit, how I was sculpted from nothing into something. Like an open book, you watched me grow from conception to birth; all the stages of my life were spread out before you, the days of my life all prepared before I'd even lived one day.[12]

That means God watched over our construction from toes to fingertips to hair roots, and he has designed each of us to be exquisite, unequaled, and beyond compare. But it will always be our choice to live our lives as ourselves—not as someone we're not.

I once read a wise phrase that stated, "Never forget you are unique—just like everyone else in the world."

That made me smile. Because truly every woman longs to be

loved just as she is. She longs to be cherished (David Cassidy sang about this word in the mid-seventies, and it still rings in my head. To *cherish* is to care about deeply.) Indeed, every woman—you, me, the "other" woman from the pages of *Teen* magazine and the one sitting next to you on the commuter train back home—longs to be cared about. We all long for our value, our worth to be based on our true self alone. The true self that's beneath, as we discovered in the last chapter, all those layers of phyllo dough. It's that core—who we truly are—that we long for others to know, and accept.

And yet sometimes we're scared to start peeling those layers off—before God, before a friend, before a counselor—even before ourselves. Why? I think the problem is that some of us have yet to be convinced that we *deserve* such love, such acceptance. Some of us have yet to accept such truth about ourselves and the dry, arid places of our lives.

And that's what we'll tackle and chat about in the next chapter.

✳ 10 ✳

SCORCHED PLACES

I was three years old when I lost my two older sisters.

Peering around the protective body of our foster mother ("Aunt Bonnie"), I watched as two strangers—a man and a woman—escorted five-year-old Lynn and four-year-old Beth* to a car softly idling in the driveway.

Moments before, while Aunt Bonnie knelt on the living room floor and gently pried apart our intertwined fingers, I had listened as the strangers promised my sisters, but not me, a hamburger and ice cream as soon as they got in the car.

I was holding on to those fingers for dear life. My preschool heart knew something was wrong—terribly wrong. It knew that in letting go, I was to lose something of great value. Yet what power does a child hold against a world of adults and social services?

Bit by bit, our fingers lost contact. Bit by bit the warmth of my sisters' hands was lost, until finally, I stood alone—my own hands clasped to my sides as I gazed through the living-room window. Staring as the only two sisters I had ever known were driven out of my life.

---

*Not their real names.

I had absolutely no control over the events that transpired from 1965 to 1968. Nor did I have control over the family I was born into. Or the marital struggles and personal battles that my birth father and mother warred against. I could have sooner lassoed a tornado than have prevented the devastating break-down and breakup of my family of origin.

In three short years of life, I had experienced the loss of a total of five biological siblings through foster care and adoption. My two brothers remained together and were adopted together as siblings, as were Lynn and Beth. My eldest sister, well into her teens, had chosen to live with extended birth family while I, the youngest child, was the last to find a new home and a family.

I've always known that I was adopted and that the entire community of Brunswick, Missouri, embraced the dark-haired daughter of Norman and Jean Patrick from the moment I first arrived. In fact, a "toddler" shower was given in my honor. And photographs attest to the generous outpouring of friends and neighbors within my hometown. I clearly remember "feeling" prized and treasured as a daughter. I had a home. I was loved.

But throughout my childhood and teen years, I would often find myself overwhelmed with what I can only describe as a "soul ache." I recall listening to a record album of the Disney movie *Mary Poppins* and crying to the lyrics of "Feed the Birds." A few years later I'd be thrown into a melancholy frame of mind by the Barry Manilow song "Mandy." And this despite my having been told that he was singing about missing his dog!

Something in the music—something in the words—spoke to that ache, and I would find myself thinking about Lynn and Beth. Although I desperately tried to remember their faces, as each year passed I was able to come up with fewer and fewer memories. I would think of my brothers, whom I couldn't remember at all, and of my older sister, Debbie, whom I learned died the summer of my thirteenth year. I thought of my birth parents, of extended family I never knew—grandparents, aunts, uncles, and cousins—and I missed them. I mourned the fact that they would never be a part of my life.

And then I'd feel guilty.

REAL guilty.

I'd berate myself with the mental accusations I had come to embrace as an adoptee.

How dare I have such feelings! After all, I had been chosen by my parents. I had been lucky enough to find a great home with a mom and dad who wanted me to be a part of their lives. Who was I to feel shortchanged? I had been given just about anything a girl could want. Who was I to miss a birth mother and birth father who had willfully signed over parental rights to their five children?

I'd look around my bedroom—filled with mementos of family vacations, school activities, and celebrations—and tell myself that I was selfish and ungrateful.

Who was I to feel such loneliness when Mom and Dad repeatedly told me how much they loved me, and I could see with my own eyes and feel with my own heart that it was true? Who was I to grow maudlin over events that had been out of my control? Who was I to long for more than I had already been given—to long for what I could never be?

And so an emotional cycle of sadness, longing, aching, and denial began. Pushed aside with a determined "Think Happy" mentality, the barrenness of my soul was swallowed up with a determined air of independence and self-preservation, and a myriad of emotions was squelched, underconsidered, and seldom spoken of to anyone around me.

But in the quiet of the night, when I was safely tucked between crisp cotton sheets with the safe, warm light of the kitchen softly casting its beam across my carpeted bedroom floor, my heart would inquire, *Whose hands do I have?*

An odd question, you may think. Yet consider this. If you are the biological relative of your father or mother, brother or sister, take the time to look at your hands. Notice the shape of your fingernails—their length, the strength or brittleness of their makeup. Consider the overall design of your hands: the knuckle size, skin texture, even the subtle moon-shaped crescent of the nail bed. Consider and compare. I believe you will note some striking similarities between yours and those of your family members. For years I have been intrigued by people's hands, and for as long I've often wondered, *Whose hands do I have?*

My birth mother's?

Or perhaps father's?

Did Lynn and Beth share the same thin, peeling nails as me?

Were their fingers slim and petite?

Did my hands look like anyone else's?

What my inner recesses demanded to know—what my adopted soul questioned and sought assurance for, despite the security of my home and the unassailable love of those in it— was confirmation that *I mattered.*

My soul, my heart, my emotions, my self-esteem, my *very being,* needed to believe—was desperate to believe—that some- where in the world there were others looking at their hands.

Looking, remembering, and still wondering about a brown-eyed, brown-haired three-year-old named Julie.

And from talking with scores of women, I know I'm not the only one who feels this way. Each of us has an unfolding story, constructed of past issues from things that are not of our choosing. Each of us, granted the time and the courage, could expose multiple layers of past and present neediness, triumphs, and losses. Each of us could testify to deeply hidden, deftly avoided scorched places of the soul.

Adoption is my story—my scorched place.

Losing contact with my brothers and sisters, diminishing the magnitude of their loss from my life, and deflecting profound insecurities that sprang up over the years helped create a vacuum of sorts in my life. An emotional, relational, spiritual, and sexual void that I sought not so much to fill but to tranquilize, to contain—to control.

And I did so (quite effectively) for nearly twenty-four years.

The power of humor and the heady rush of being center stage and the life of the party carried me through junior and senior high school. I fought the proverbial allure of alcohol and sex (with varying degrees of success and/or failure) and, during my college years, immersed myself in the Christian faith that I had embraced as a nine-year-old girl.

I married six months after college graduation and found myself pregnant within weeks of the honeymoon. From the moment I knew of my first child's existence to the birth of our third and final child in 1995, I was blissfully preoccupied—unable and unwilling to deal with the vacuum that was becoming increasingly difficult to satisfy or fill.

But hiding from one's past is never safe for the soul. And so I found myself dealing with parental anger and rage in my late twenties—acting out toward my children in ways that terrified and shamed me. And thinking even darker thoughts that I could scarcely admit to myself, let alone to my husband or friends.

In my early thirties I began to experience debilitating fatigue. My mind seemed to be muddled—cloudy—unable to multitask with the pinpoint accuracy I had come to depend on over the years. I'd be in the middle of a conversation and completely blank out—I'd have no idea what I had just said or what point I was attempting to make. My right foot began to feel numb, and when I shaved my calf to the top of my kneecap, there was an odd, hard-to-describe, desensitized sensation.

I found myself craving sleep—becoming addicted to its anes-thetizing power. I would send the children off to school at 7:45 A.M. and crawl back into bed or lie on the couch until 1:00 P.M. Then I'd hurriedly shower, put on makeup, and attempt to "do" something that would prove to my family that I had been alive and functioning while they were absent.

Day after day, month after month, this scenario played out. My children began to comment on my lack of involvement with them. My husband noted that I seldom left the house or seemed to care about the things I had once enjoyed—entertaining friends and family or shopping for fun stuff at Target.

I gained weight. My sexual drive, which had been healthy and robust up to then, was a flat line on the screen of marriage. And I felt bad about all of those things. I didn't want to *be* this way, but I found it impossible to "think" my way, or "purpose" my way, or "just change" the way I felt and acted.

My friends, I was at the end of my rope. And one morning, while lying back in bed, I acknowledged a thought that had been moving under the radar for weeks: *I wish I could cover up my head and go to sleep forever.*

I wanted to die.

To this day it is difficult to acknowledge the suicidal feelings I was having that morning. My tendency is to cloak them with a veneer of palpable verbiage—to put such a personal spin on it all that it sounds less than it truly was. But the truth is, I was in a deep, dark place. Depression hung like a gray cloak over my shoulders. It had fed on the arid places of my soul, my memories, and my present, rendering me helpless for the first time in my life.

It was a place where I never expected to be. After all, I was Julie, the one who made everyone laugh. The one who made fun out of the "little things" of life. Who, in general, had always sucked "the marrow out of life," to quote the movie *Dead Poets Society.* Even more, I was Julie the Christian, who had until that morning never imagined thinking such black thoughts. But I did, my friend, I did. I had not walked away from my faith. I hadn't somehow lost my salvation on the road of depression. Nor had God turned his head in disgust at the sight of me curled up in bed, attempting to avoid the life he had orchestrated. I was simply battling very real and very human emotions and my Christian status didn't make me impervious to them.

That dark period in my life showed me that all of us—regardless of our background, age, or social status—have needs, wants, *scorched places* that only divine grace can reach. We've all been burned by events and circumstances over which we have no control. For you, the scorched place may be a lack of parental affection or presence, verbal or sexual abuse, divorce, the betrayal of a friendship, mental illness, physical handicaps, limited financial funds, or any countless other wounds.

The reality is this: Without the power of God imparting kindness, mercy, and favor to my most painful wounds, I would have never been able to extricate myself from those shameful thoughts, emotions, and possible actions. It was (and continues to be) grace, illuminating the shadows of depressive darkness, which unleashed a cacophony of change and healing for my life. It was supernatural grace, coupled with the practical, medicinal, grace of antidepressants, which brought about my ultimate healing. I believe, without shame or hesitancy, that God directs physicians and pharmacists as sovereignly as he does pastors and Christian authors! His lavish grace-giving is not limited to the ethereal but is evidenced in the very chemical compounds of our bodies and medicinal aids.

God desires for us to be complete in every facet of our makeup, and who better than our Creator to lead us in that journey?!

> Long before he laid down earth's foundations, he had us in mind, had settled on us as the focus of his love, to be made whole and holy by his love. Long, long ago he decided to adopt us into his family through Jesus Christ. (What pleasure he took in planning this!) He wanted us to enter into the celebration of his lavish gift-giving by the hand of his beloved Son.[13]

How those words resonate within my adopted soul! Resonate and revive the hurting places that only his divine grace can reach.

The Creator of this earth—your Creator—longs for your scorched places to be healed, to be nourished, to be fed by springs of water that never fail or run dry. He desires for you to be refreshed in these most painful of places simply because he loves you. And he offers encouragement and hope: "I will always show you where to go. I'll give you a full life in the emptiest of places—firm muscles, strong bones. You'll be like a well-watered garden, a gurgling spring that never runs dry."[14]

And if that isn't audacious enough, he goes on to promise that it will be the very rubble, the broken fragment of your life, that he will use to build anew the foundations of your past.[15]

Oh, how I desire that! To have the broken places rebuilt. To be restored. To know that even the uncontrollable parts of my past can be used in the restoration process of life.

Years ago I heard writer Maya Angelou quote an African proverb that in essence said, "I *see* you—not only am I looking at you, but I see your true authentic self."

Every woman and every little girl inside that woman longs to be seen and known. In our woundedness we ache for someone to look us in the eye and with unwavering gaze tell us, "I see you."

You.

The woman behind the masks and the hang-ups.

Your heart.

Your desires.

Your dreams. As well as the shattered illusions that have come crumbling and crashing down around you.

I *see* you.

The eyes of Scandalous Divine Grace saw:

✳ An abandoned three-year-old who watched her sisters leave.

✳ A teenage girl garnering attention and affection through joke-telling and flirting.

✳ A twenty-something mother of two children under age two, slowly coming apart at her contrived seams.

✳ A broken and heartsick thirty-year-old, depressed and ready to quit.

And so Grace sees you . . . in all your scorched places too. And longs to fill the vacuum of your heart.

GOT GUILT?

Well, of course we do. We're female, aren't we?

That friendly little guy's voice from AOL keeps popping up on the screen of life announcing, "You've Got Guilt!" . . . for all sorts of things. Things you've said. Things you've done. Emotions you've felt. Actions you've taken.

And guilt for things you didn't say. Things you didn't do. Emotions you didn't feel—or didn't feel "correctly." And actions you didn't take.

"Guilt," columnist Erma Bombeck once observed, is "the gift that keeps on giving." Giving us headaches, worries, fears, regrets, ulcers . . . and, of course, more guilt.

I almost feel guilty writing about guilt. After all, if you've read more than, oh, let's say, three books in the past ten years that were geared toward women, you have, in all probability, read a chapter about guilt.

"Good" guilt.

"Bad" guilt.

"True" guilt.

"False" guilt.

"Survivor" guilt.

"Healthy" guilt.

"Pathological" guilt.

"Unconscious" guilt.

As well as the ever delightful "anticipatory" guilt, for those of us who can't help but think of all the things we'll feel guilty about—tomorrow.

Ah, so much guilt, so little time.

A quick search on Amazon.com resulted in 682 title hits for the keyword *guilt.* I believe I've read 598 of them. Well, I've purchased that many, but I haven't actually found time to read them all. *(Hmm, all that money spent, all that wisdom just waiting to be gleaned . . . it's starting to make me feel . . . guilty!)* Anyway, those books are tucked neatly on dusty shelves, pushed beneath a bed, or stacked on an ever-burgeoning pile of material on a wobbly nightstand. And guess what? I still wrestle with the rascally subject of guilt.

In an effort to alleviate a small portion of anticipatory guilt, I'm going to do something a little different as an author writing about the subject. Instead of hitting you with an avalanche of Internet information (suspect at best) and factoids or trying to convince you that I understand the plethora of psychological aspects in regards to guilt, I'm simply going to share with you some of the pit stops my girlfriends and I have traversed in our own journeys of scandalous grace.

PORT OF CALL: THE LAND OF PAST CHOICES

I've made some pretty lousy choices in my life. *(I'd call them "stupid" choices, but 481 of the aforementioned books said you shouldn't do that.)* Lousy choices, then—pretty dumb choices, if I may speak frankly.

There was the time that I, at the age of sixteen, attempted to parallel park my parents' Chevy Impala at a high school baseball game and chose to ask my friend Kathy Harke if there was enough space between the two cars ahead and behind me to park in between. I chose to believe her when she yelled to me from her line of vision, "Plenty . . . you've got plenty of room!" I chose to put the car in reverse and to move rather quickly into the plentiful space.

Then I heard a horrific scraping noise.

I chose to put the car in drive and accelerate.

Another more horrific noise.

I then chose to put the car back in reverse and see if I could figure out what the problem was. *(Pure genius, I know.)*

Again the scraping.

Again my pulling forward until at last I jumped out of the driver's side and ran around to the passenger portion. I chose to believe that I had not caved in the entire right flank of the family car.

But guess what? Those examples aren't even the stupidest— I meant to say, *lousiest*—choices that I made in this entire story. No, those were all still to come.

Gathering around me was nearly the entire high school baseball team. Impressed with my driving skills, they cheered me on as I drove away, wondering how on earth I was going to explain this to my parents.

Ever since the knickers incident, I had been prone to weasel my way out of things. And this was to be no different. Pulling into the familiar drive on Buchanan Street, I parked the car as far from the house as possible and started to scheme. My father was at the Lake of the Ozarks in southern Missouri, so I knew it was Mom I was going to have to face. I gathered my wits about me and walked into the house.

"Mom," I yelled, "can you come outside? I have something to show you."

She came out from the family room and followed me to the driveway. Walking her around the car, I pointed in a rather dramatic fashion and wailed, "Look what happened at the park!"

She was stunned.

Amazed.

Hacked off.

"How did you do this to the car, Julie?" And she waited for my answer.

Now I could have chosen any number of things to say. One being the truth. But that really wasn't my style as a teenage girl wanting to keep her driving privileges. So I chose to say instead, "I don't know! I parked the car, and when I came back to come home . . . THIS" —another dramatic hand motion to the crumpled side—"was there."

It just came out. Those words. And they hung there in the air. *Will she buy it?* I wondered.

Mom stared at the car again. Watching her expressions, I believed I caught a tiny glimpse of acceptance. Then, looking me straight in the eye she responded, "Well, we're going to have to report this to the sheriff! There had to be witnesses. You were at the park for the varsity baseball game—someone had to see what happened. We'll just call Perry *(when you live in a small town, you call the local sheriff by his first name)* and file a report."

Well . . . that wasn't quite what I had expected. And I could see larger trouble gathering down the road.

Therefore, within a matter of seconds, I heard myself confessing the truth, confessing that I had lied, and confessing that I was a miserable excuse for a daughter and didn't deserve ever to be trusted with the car again.

One more bad choice.

My dad concurred with the part about being trusted with the car. It was a good month or more before I was allowed to get behind the wheel of the Impala again. And another two or three before I could turn over the ignition.

We all have made lousy choices. Some can be laughed at *(at least I can laugh; my parents still don't find that story all that amusing)*. Others, well . . . they are far more serious choices, and the guilt we feel as a result of making them may seem like it will never go away. All too often, we find ourselves in a painful cycle of making poor decisions based on our residual feelings about our past choices.

Choices to lie, steal, or deceive.

Choices to go against our better judgment. To forego our personal convictions or not stand by our beliefs.

Choices to compromise. We've all made *those* choices and could probably rattle them off to one another with ease.

Guilt travels on the back of past choice . . . and loves to attach itself to our second port of call.

PORT OF CALL: THE CONTINENT OF PAST REGRETS

This area of guilt is so vast it merits its own zip code. Traveling through the continent of past regrets we come face-to-face with the choices we have made in every area of our life. And none of those choices seem to affect us as deeply as the sexual choices we make. The guilt and regret eat away at our heart, pollute our memory, and systemically decimate the innermost spiritual part of who we are as women.

Unforgiven and unreleased sexual regrets will act as toxins in your life—ignored and unattended, they will fester and eventually poison the sexual design that God himself invented and declared good.

This is another scorched place that many of us are living with—inwardly dying with—but are too ashamed to confess or too afraid to trust anyone with the details. I've spoken with hundreds of women, and more via E-mail, and many are warring with the guilt of premarital sex. Most of these women are married—often to the man they had sex with before the rings were exchanged—and many of them are stunned to find that five, ten, fifteen years down the road of matrimony, they are still tied up with regret over the choice they made years earlier.

This regret often surprises them—especially those who grew up post-sexual revolution and may not have considered premarital sex that big of a deal. Oftentimes the acknowledgment of this residual guilt comes at a time when their oldest child is approaching puberty. There's something about hearing your son's voice changing, seeing hair peeking over his lip, or watching the development of your daughter's hips and breasts that brings out the instinctive urge to protect and shelter them from the fallout of sexual choices—the fallout and regrets that you yourself live with.

But women don't simply carry regret and guilt for sexual choices from the past. They are burdened with the choices they have made (or are making) in the present—as Christians.

Whew, we're diving in deep now. Look, the reality is that some of us are toying with sexual infidelity. Some of us are engaged in, if not a physical, then an emotional affair of the mind and heart—with men who are not our spouses. And we can barely see our way clear of the guilt and regret.

We know it's wrong.

We know the Bible verses that say it's wrong.

And yet . . . we find ourselves drawn to him.

His wit.

His humor.

His ability to appreciate the work we do.

His "you're totally *not* like my husband" characteristics.

I know a woman who is caught in such a place. She has told me of the way a certain man makes her heart sing whenever she hears his voice. She has told me of their correspondence and of their "chemistry" that is impossible to dismiss.

And she has wept with me as we have talked out this scenario to its logical, bitter end. Talked out the details of her choosing to consummate the chemistry. About how she might feel twelve hours after that encounter. Talked about her husband finding out. About the look on his face as he learns of her betrayal. About the anger and rage that would be sure to follow. And about her facing her children, ages nine and four, and explaining to them that Mommy would not be living with Daddy anymore.

And then we have wept. And prayed—oh, how we have prayed.

You would never imagine—from the outside looking in—that my friend could be engaged in such a battle. After all, she teaches a weekly Bible class, she attends a well-respected church, and she loves Jesus. She really does love Jesus. But still the struggle. Still the fight.

Others reading these words are single—single and frustrated! Brave writer (and girlfriend material for sure) Shea Gregory writes in her witty and poignant article "Confessions of a Sex-Starved Single" of her own battles with urges and raging hormones:

> [My friend] Diane says I think about sex too much and must learn to master my bodily urges. I tell her I'd rather let a man do that. She says I'm carnal. I say I'm passionate. She says I must wait on God. I tell her I think God's watch must be broken because he's running a bit late. She says I'm silly because God invented time and doesn't even need a watch. I hate it when she gets theological on me.[16]

Married, single, or divorced, there is truth that we all need to hear at this point: God knows about our struggle. After all, he made us. He's not surprised (or disgusted) by the sexual needs that we have as women.

Neither is he surprised by any of your sins. There really is nothing new under the sun. The Internet may allow us access to images and addictions that we never imagined ourselves fighting, but God has seen the devastating allure of pornography destroy lives before. Trashy novels filled with sexual exploits may hold sway over your thoughts and govern fantasies that no one knows about. But God has seen others walk the treacherous path you are on. There is *nothing* hidden from him. And that is our salvation! We can revel in this biblical truth: It is by God's grace alone that we are saved from sin and ourselves!

> You let the world, which doesn't know the first thing about living, tell you how to live. You filled your lungs with polluted unbelief, and then exhaled disobedience. We all did it, all of us doing what we felt like doing, when we felt like doing it, all of us in the same boat. It's a wonder God didn't lose his temper and do away with the whole lot of us. Instead, immense in mercy and with an incredible love, he embraced us. He took our sin-dead lives and made us alive in Christ. He did all this on his own, with no help from us![17]

FINAL PORT OF CALL: THE WONDERLAND OF GRACE

God knows that we are sometimes weak, sometimes strong, and sometimes unfaithful to the vows and commitments we have made to him and others. And he understands, better than any one of us ever will, that without his supernatural grace and power to forgive and renew our hearts and minds, we will never win this battle—on any front.

Maybe you can identify with these words that summarize so aptly the place we find ourselves all too many times: "What I don't understand about myself is that I decide one way, but then I act another, doing things I absolutely despise."[18]

The scandalous love of God understands that we are weak.

The scandalous grace of God offers forgiveness each and every time.

The scandalous work of God restores putrid places of the mind, the heart, and the body to palaces of purity. And it renews within us—through his Holy Spirit—a desire to walk the walk, sleep the sleep, and talk the talk that we all long to be faithful to.

All that's left for us to do is confess and receive.

So confess the sexual sins that separate you from your Creator, your spouse, your conscience, and your faith. Confess them and know this: "If we give up on him, he does not give up—for there's no way he can be false to himself."[19] What does this mean? God is faithful. Over and over again. And you can never out-sin or out-choose or out-regret his mercy and grace.

✳ 12 ✳

ℒILY PADS

𝒪n her nationally best-selling book *Traveling Mercies,* author Anne Lamott writes,

> My coming to faith did not start with a leap but rather a series of staggers from what seemed like one safe place to another. Like lily pads, round and green, these places summoned me and then held me up while I grew. Each prepared me for the next leaf on which I would land, and in this way I moved across the swamp of doubt and fear. When I look back at some of these early resting places— the boisterous home of the Catholics, the soft armchair of the Christian Science mom, adoption by ardent Jews— I can see how flimsy and indirect a path they made. Yet each step brought me closer to the verdant pad of faith on which I somehow stay afloat today.[20]

I have memorized these lines, for they speak to my heart and articulate with a writing grace I've yet to possess, the complex—yet blessedly simple—truth of faith, life, and the wonder of the divine. It is my nature to document the ins and outs of life. To record for posterity's sake the good, the bad, and the ugly concerning my life and the world around me.

I have never met a journal I didn't like. Nor been able to ignore a five-pack special of yellow legal pads.

I have a diary from fifth grade. It seems I embraced scandalous living even then. I found a notation that explained how I had been sent to the principal's office after my fifth-grade teacher had confiscated a copy of *Love's Avenging Heart,* which I had brought with me to class—with all the "good" parts underlined in red.

Come to think of it, I have dozens of high school, college, and adult ramblings written in all sorts of journals, diaries, notebooks, and yellow pads.

Upon the worst-case scenario of our house burning, I have instructed all family members to get themselves and at least three legal pads out to safety. You see, my life can be pieced together, bound, and sold, from the myriad of writings, ramblings, and notes lying about my home. These pieces of pressed tree pulp and ink present tangible evidence that I have lived.

Lived and loved.

Lived and lost.

Lived and made a way across my swamps of fear and doubt.

As I look back on that evidence, as I read and remember the places I have been, the things I have done, and the people I have seen, it is the unshakable presence of women—girlfriends—who have been the "lily pads of grace" that have held, supported, and launched my own journey of faith and life.

And I don't mean just *friends.* I mean *girlfriends.* Now it's imperative that we recognize the vast difference between a *friend* and a *girlfriend.* The two are not the same. Comparing the two—and declaring them equal—would be as preposterous as claiming that filet mignon and tenderized chuck steak are the same cut of beef. *(Is it just me, or is food a very symbolic thing in my life?)* Considering *friend* and *girlfriend* to be one and the same is as ridiculous as eating celery to balance the effects of too much chocolate in one's diet! Being someone's friend is not the same as being someone's girlfriend.

No, there is a huge difference. And one that women every-where can relate to. There are friends, and there are girlfriends. Pure and simple. If it pleases the court . . .

EXHIBIT E: EXAMPLES

✳ A friend will ask, "Are you wearing that dress tonight?"

✳ A girlfriend will ask, "You are *not* wearing that dress tonight . . . are you?"

✳ You go to work with a friend.

✳ You "work it" with a girlfriend!

Oh yes, the memories of being single and with my girls! Cruising in a sporty car, radio blasting with Bryan Adams wailing away, and laughing my head off as Cindy and Shelly try to get the attention of the male driver of a Ford pickup behind us.

And you don't stop working it with the girlfriends just because you're married. It just morphs into a different kind of "work it."

About three years ago, I piled Margie, Kate, and Toni into my sporty 1990 Lumina. (I mentioned said vehicle in the opening salvo of the book.) *At the time, the only thing that worked on the van was the ignition key. A rubber bumper strip had fallen off the right side and had left a lovely glue spot down the entire side. The front passenger door had to be opened from the inside, and the interior dome lights did not work. And, should I wish to load a cart full of groceries through the rear hatch, I would first need to climb over the second- and third-row seating and pop it open from the interior.*

THAT was the vehicle my girlfriends piled into—with little complaint. We then proceeded to crank up the radio, listened to the classic rock sounds of Journey, and cruised around the city of Galesburg, Illinois.

Yes, I said cruised. Downtown we went, pulling up next to a souped-up piece of vehicular art. I looked at the eleven-year-old driver (maybe it was just me who thought that), revved my engine, and visually challenged him to a runoff. My girls were dying—from embarrassment and laughter! I peeled out and made my way to the bank parking lot, where all hormonally active teens hang out. Pulling into the drive, I rolled down my window and shouted to no one in particu-lar, "Hey, your mom called and said it was time you were getting home!"

Then I laughed so hard and sang so loud with eighties favorite, Journey and Steve Perry, that I lost my voice the next day. Now THAT, my girlfriend, is the difference between working with a friend and working it with your girlfriends!

✳ You eat dinner with your friend.

✳ You eat off the plate of your girlfriend.

If you're unsure as to where you stand with a particular woman—maybe you feel half friends, half girlfriends— I suggest you take her out to eat. Somewhere like the Olive Garden or something. Take her out, and when both your meals arrive, look over at hers and say, "Oh, yours looks so much better than mine," and then take your fork and move toward the main entrée. If she's a friend, you'll draw back a mangled stub. If a girlfriend, she'll offer you a bite of the side dish too.

Are you picking up on the subtle—and not so subtle—distinctions between the two? Here are a few more "Girlfriend Facts" to help.

TOP GIRLFRIEND FACTS

1. Girlfriends stop competing at some point in time. Can you remember being a teenager and preparing for a big event like a banquet, dance, homecoming, or prom? Can you remember what your chief concern—after finding the perfect dress or gown to wear—was? In my *Smallville* world of friendship, it was this: to be thinner than everyone else and have the dress with the biggest "Wow!" factor. Simply put, I wanted to beat my friends. I was competing.

But then something glorious happened. It was around the time I turned thirty *(see chapter 2)*. Seemingly overnight I went from being a competitive friend to an "Eh, you win, I give up" girlfriend. I no longer felt compelled to "top" the women in my life. I no longer felt the need to starve myself (three-day fasts from eating Hostess Ho Hos) in order to be as slim as Lisa Hirtzel. Now that was some liberating grace happening in my life, girlfriends!

2. Girlfriends will keep the child no one else—not even its grandparents—wants. You've won a trip to the Bahamas. It's just you and a spouse or a girlfriend who can get away, traveling to the shores of sunshine and blissfulness. But in the meantime, you have to find a place for your children to stay. Your two, three, or more children. And all of them are easy to dole out—all of them but the one. The one who sparks terror in the hearts of his tired grandparents. The one who rises at 5:00 A.M. and stops around 11:45 P.M. That one.

And just about the time you think you're going to have to cancel your getaway, the phone rings. It's another girlfriend, one who can't get away, and she says, "Hey, I hear you're going to the Bahamas. Whooo-ha! Do you need me to watch Junior for you?"

And as your heart breaks into a million pieces, you promise to bring her back some overpriced beach paraphernalia from the shores of tropical bliss.

3. Girlfriends do not keep a record of the years you've neglected to send a birthday or Christmas card. See, a friend will allow you two—maybe three—vacancies in this department. Then after that, I'm sorry, but it's all over. You are officially taken OFF THE LIST. With a mere flick of a key or the touch of a stylus, you are gone!

Girlfriends don't need this additional pressure. Girlfriends know that it means JUST AS MUCH if you pick up the phone, oh, let's say around February 19, and wish each other a Merry Christmas. Girlfriends know that a Reese's peanut butter cup purchased during a marathon human resources–symposium and slid across a table with the whispered words, "You look hungry," means as much as a birthday card. Girlfriends know.

4. Girlfriends torment you by getting you laughing in highly inappropriate places. I attended American History class in college with my girlfriends Lisa Clark and Lesa Ward. We were inseparable. One could barely go to the bathroom without the other two lagging behind. We clicked in every way you can imagine.

We had each auditioned for and played a specific part in the threesome we shared:

- * Julie Patrick: comedienne and a bit flighty
- * Lisa Clark: eternal optimist and the ultimate tenderheart
- * Lesa Ward: instigator and group loan officer (she always had money!)

We worked well together—sometimes too well. Like the time Lesa W. wrote a note critiquing a certain hairstyle of a classmate seated in front of us. This struck a nerve—a humor nerve—and I began to laugh. Just slightly. Under my breath. No one could even tell.

Then Lisa C. wrote a follow-up note that elaborated on said hairstyle. I then snorted aloud. Once, twice, three times. Snorted and covered my mouth in a vain attempt to quell my laughter.

Lesa W. then said something under her breath—and I lost it completely. I guffawed right in the middle of Professor Powell's stunning dissertation on the ramifications of the Marshall Plan. Girlfriends can say one word, or glance at you with "that" look, and send you spurting out of control.

5. Girlfriends don't talk behind your back. They say exactly what they think to your face. Enough said?

6. Girlfriends are there for you in an instant. Geographical distance doesn't matter, if you are close in heart. And when you really need them, they go the distance—whether long hours on the phone or an impromptu visit "just because you sound like you need it."

7. Girlfriends have learned that life is an incredible road of joys and sorrows. They know, through their own life experiences, that all the pieces of life sometimes don't fit. As hard as you try to make them fit. And girlfriends know they need one another more than they had ever imagined.

I think it does our heart and mind good to look back and consider the journey we have already walked and the women who made that journey possible. So now I want you to consider the "lily pads" of girlfriend grace that God has allowed in your life.

Can you recall your first true girlfriend? In all likelihood she was a friend who at some distinct point and time acted in such a manner that she shifted into the girlfriend category for life.

Oftentimes that "act" was one of self-sacrifice—something that showed you how much she cared for you.

I can tell you in a snap who my first girlfriend was. Her name was Shelly Tate. Shelly Tate Kussman now, twenty-odd years down the track. I was raised in a small community of 1,200 or so people. I went to school, K–12, with the same boys and girls. There were twenty-two of us in our high school graduating class. So I knew Shelly from the get-go. We were in elementary classes together. And together we terrorized poor Mrs. Volk in the sixth year of our academic pursuits. Shelly was a friend for all those years. We sat together at lunch, she picked me to be on her kickball team, and we both were invited to each other's birthday parties. But it wasn't until the fall of my seventh-grade year that Shelly came to be a girlfriend.

We were in our seventh-grade math class with . . . oh, let's just refer to her as Ms. Attila the Hun. This was the season of "New Math." And daily we were told that the entire United States would be converting to metric measurements. That meant that if you didn't know the metric system by the spring of that year, well, you were doomed.

I believed it all. Hook, line, and sinker. I remember thinking that I would be unable to cook for my family as an adult. After all, how would I ever be able to measure liquids if I didn't understand metric measurements? I was doomed, all right—and so were my poor husband and children-to-be.

I tried to understand all the *mm* (millimeter) and *cm* (centimeter) and other meter stuff, but my brain just wasn't cooperating. It embarrassed me. Being such a dunce in math was even worse because so many of my friends (Shelly included) seemed to breeze through without a problem. So I came to dread that fourth-hour math class, especially when papers were returned and commented on loudly by Ms. Attila the Hun.

"Donna, you got an 89 percent. Good job."

"Mike has the highest grade; again he received a 98 percent. Excellent job!"

Row after row, student by student, Ms. Attila the Hun would exclaim about her students' progress.

And then it would be my turn to be recognized. . . .

Sighing with exasperation, Ms. Attila would dramatically return my test and say, "As usual, Julie, you have one of the lowest grades in the class. You really should try harder."

Now is that awful or what? *(And I gratefully appreciate your expressions of outrage and sympathy.)*

"You really should try harder." That's the line that killed me. Because I *was* trying, as hard as I could. My parents had even hired a tutor for me after school hours. I sat at the dining-room table with Dad, night after night, trying to convert numbers and measurements. I *was* trying! And I didn't think it was even possible to try any harder!

So on this particular occasion, I responded in the manner befitting a humiliated seventh-grade girl. I began to bawl. I'm talking not just a tear or two, but the sobbing, gut-wrenching, snot-running-down-my-face bawling. I'm talking wailing, renting-the-fabric-of-my-garments bawling.

My classmates sat in stunned silence.

Ms. Attila, walking back to her desk, commented just under her breath, "Oh, grow up."

That's when the metamorphosis occurred.

Standing to her feet, three seats behind me, my friend Shelly Tate spoke with a quavering voice. "You are so mean to Julie! You should be ashamed of yourself for making her cry!"

The pin dropped and everyone heard it.

Ms. Attila stared at Shelly—speechless.

I blew my nose, stood up, and went and hugged my *girlfriend* Shelly. From that day forth and forevermore, she was *girlfriend* Shelly. She had taken a risk *(I don't believe Ms. Attila ever read grades out loud again after that)* and had revealed her magnificent girlfriend-heart to me and everyone in that classroom.

She was one of the first "lily pads" of girlfriend grace that I can remember. Who's yours?

Can you recall your first "substitute sister" girlfriend? She's the sister you wish you had. Since I'd lost three sisters through adoption, as you might expect I was always looking for someone to fill that empty place in my life. And my forever and always "I wish you were my sister" will always be Cindy Jo Johnson.

She and I first became "sisters" as first-graders in Mrs. Starks's class. I'm not even sure Cindy remembers this, but one day I wet my pants in that class. It was Cindy who dropped a Kleenex or two in my direction, helping me clean up the embarrassing mess before someone noticed.

I have a charm bracelet that my mother started for me in 1971, and linked to that chain are three or four charms, engraved with the words *Best friends—Cindy.*

I loved Cindy with all my heart and enjoyed nothing more

than going to her house and hanging out with her and her four sisters.

Now, some of you who have siblings may be thinking, *I can remember the sibling I wish wasn't my sibling!* And that's the kind of atmosphere I enjoyed at Cindy's house. Her three older sisters—Kay, Gerry Anne, and Lynda—were forever fighting and yelling about something. They would express their sorrow in one another's existence and argue about sweaters worn without permission and mascara left without the cap being screwed back on.

I have to tell you: I loved it! I reveled in it all. I would plop myself square in the center of Cindy's bed, which was covered with an aqua blue comforter, and just take in the show. I would have given anything to have been a "Johnson girl" at that time. And it was the hand and finger shape of Kay, Gerry, Lynda, and Cindy's hands that first impacted the scorched places of my adopted soul.

I can tell you—twenty years down the road now—that I still enjoy making my way up the steps to Cindy's childhood home. I still enjoy hearing her update me on all that they are doing, and I can assure you that the sisters no longer scream in a fevered pitch at one another. They have settled into an enviable relationship of love, acceptance, and family connection.

And Cindy will always be the sister I wish I'd had.

Lily pads of girlfriend connections come in a variety of packages.

Some are landing pads—a brief layover on our way to the next divinely directed woman in our life.

Others act as launching pads—propelling us onward toward the goal of our hearts and dreams.

And a few become the keepers of our secrets—the confidantes of all that could destroy us. Yet we rest, knowing that apart from God, there is no one more trustworthy.

It has been the verdant, growing relationships between girlfriends and me that have saved me from the scorched places, expanded my oft protracted sense of self, and brought me across the swamp of fear and doubt.

And these same girlfriends have also accompanied me to the streams of living water, encouraging and enabling me to drink from the depths of all that is divine and true. For it is through those girlfriends—who have often acted toward me as instruments of God's love and mercy—that I have been able to taste, touch, and feel more of God's scandalous grace.

Cindy, childhood friend and "substitute sister" girlfriend, has seen me at my pontificating, overzealous worst—and has chosen to hang in there with me as I stumble and attempt to articulate with grace this faith journey I find myself traveling. Anne has forgiven my not-so-much breaking, but painfully bending of the parameters of confidentiality and has gloriously allowed me to share her confidence once more. Audrey knows the ugliest truths about me—and has never used them as a weapon against me. Such love! Such grace! And while they may not be aware of it, each of them has acted as a "seasoning" of grace in my life: even tempered; quick to forgive an offense; wearing the all-purpose garment of love.[21]

Without girlfriends I would be lost—and still oh, so thirsty.

* 13 *

SCANDALOUS THINKING

*C*all me crazy, but what if extending grace to ourselves and others meant that we no longer thought about things the way we used to? What if grace created a new paradigm by which we lived our lives, thought our thoughts, and acted out toward others?

Consider the "out-of-bounds" possibilities for your own life.

WHAT IF:

You woke up in the morning and never thought about your weight?
Just last night, I found a high school English composition journal from 1981. I read it out loud to my fourteen-year-old daughter and watched her reactions as she listened to the thoughts and feelings of her own mother some twenty years prior.

Here's just a sampling. . . .

March 13, 1981

Oh, my life is so hard! Boys are such a pain in the neck. They tell you one thing and do something else. Yesterday,

Science Club went to Columbia, Missouri, and visited a nuclear place. To be truthful, the only exciting thing about that was the real cute man in the control room. It wasn't too bad, but here's the thing, I am going to lose weight! I've finally got the willpower. I think. I want to lose about thirty pounds. That way I can gain five or ten and still be slim. The doctor told me that I could weigh eighty-four pounds and be okay, but I think that might be too skinny.

I had to cringe as I read the above to Kristen. Good grief! What doctor in his right mind would tell a fifteen-year-old girl she could weigh eighty-four pounds and still be okay? I was also taken aback by my declaration to "lose thirty pounds." Granted, I may have been less than svelte in 1981, but I certainly did not have thirty extra pounds to lose. And as you probably have guessed, I never even came close to doing so. As I read those words, I can feel the burden of graceless thinking on my mind and soul all over again.

Most of us can't even begin to imagine being oblivious to our weight. We buy scales, placing them in the only room of the house where we can be naked and absolutely alone—the bathroom. And those scales not only tell us our technical weight but also our body-mass index. We step on them once, twice, three, and four times a day. Gauging the hit we took from breakfast, lunch, or dinner within hours of digesting the meal.

Many of us have daughters watching—picking up on the cues we give regarding body image and self-confidence. And I'm afraid our actions are speaking louder than our words. We may "tell" them they are beautiful just the way they are. We may "tell" them that we love them regardless of their shape or curves. We may "tell" them it's what's on the inside that matters. We may say all these things, but if we are allowing the digital display on a set of scales to dictate our mood and our perception of who we—or they—truly are, then we're sounding a whole lot like Charlie Brown's teacher in the Peanuts strips: "Wah, wah, wah, wah, wah, wah."

What would it take to get you to this level of thinking—to be NOT thinking about your weight?

Would removing the scales and throwing them in the trash help? I'm thinking yes. Because if you feel comfortable in your clothes and in your own skin, does it *really* matter what those digits read? And vice versa. If you *don't* feel comfortable in your clothes or your own skin, does it matter what those digits read? Isn't it about finding the "zone" that works for you as a woman?

Here's how I have been liberated by grace in this specific area. I no longer know what I weigh. In fact, I won't even get on the scales when I go to the doctor's office! *(How's that for auda-cious!?)* I heard Dr. Nancy Snyderman on the *Oprah Winfrey Show* one time. She said there's no medical urgency in being weighed on routine visits. It's just something doctors' offices do. And she then said, "You don't have to step on the scales if you don't want to."

Hallelujah! What freedom. What grace. Because there have been times in my life when I did not go to the doctor's simply because I loathed the idea of stepping on that stupid scale. And just so you know—I did refuse to do it.

Betsy, my doctor's office nurse, was filling out information for my routine Pap test when she said, "Okay, Julie, I need to weigh you now."

I declined.

She looked at me like I was crazy. "Uh, you're not going to step on the scale?" she asked.

"That's right. I'm not going to let you weigh me. I'm not going to step on those scales. I'm just not going to do it."

"Well, okay, I'll just write down your weight as the same as last year."

A few moments—oh, who are we kidding? I was in a doctor's office!—*several* moments later, my doctor tapped on the door and tentatively entered. Smiling just a bit, he eyed me and said, "So you're refusing to be weighed. . . . Any cause for your rebellion, Julie?"

"Nope," I replied with a steely calm. "I just decided that I don't like being weighed, and if my weight should change significantly at any time, well, you'll be one of the first persons I let know."

I am woman, hear me roar!!

You walked to the clothes dryer, grabbed a pair of jeans, and before you pulled them up past your kneecaps, you HADN'T decided it was going to be a lousy day?

I'm at that awkward stage of development . . . my hips remember fitting into denim, but denim doesn't remember fitting over my hips. Sigh. I didn't mind lying down to zip my jeans when I was sixteen. But peeling the skin back on my finger as it's locked in a death struggle against my stomach—well, that just isn't my idea of fun anymore! So I've found myself shopping for "alternative" *(read "ugly")* jean wear.

Real jeans cheer, "I'm taut and youthful." Faux jeans nag, "I'm pushing middle age."

Real jeans exude vitality. Faux jeans want to go home and nap.

Real jeans hurt. Faux jeans are comfortable enough to sleep in.

Feeling your rear end following you wasn't a bad thing?

I've told this story in another book, but it's a good one and worth repeating *(if I do have to say so myself)*.

I was standing in line at the bank one summer morning with about twelve other customers and my eighteen-month-old daughter. The lobby was bustling with customers, all waiting for overstressed tellers who would have preferred to be out sunbathing rather than giving change to yet one more customer.

The banking center had an open design that made all the personal bankers privy to the comings and goings of staff and customers. In addition, the bank managers had their offices along the perimeter of the building, each enclosed with glass walls that afforded every titled employee a front-row seat to any banking spectacles, such as the one I was about to present.

I was third in line, and little Kristen was standing directly behind me. She sported a cute summer outfit with a large red strawberry motif on the shirt and tiny baby strawberries on the matching shorts. Her silky dark brown hair fell just to her shoulders and drew up into bouncy tendrils that framed her chocolate brown eyes. Her smooth olive complexion and mischievous expression caused more than one fellow spectator to exclaim, "How adorable!"

I had delivered my second child, Ricky Neal, about three weeks before, and I was sporting the appropriate clothing for one who had, until recently, been very pregnant. My oversized T-shirt, knotted loosely at my hips, strategically camouflaged the results of having carried a nine-pound, eight-ounce bundle of joy. The black, stretchy Capri leggings, accented at the calves with a wide band of lace, did their best not to give away evidence of the Oreo cookie raids preceding his birth.

While Kristen and I waited in line, she entertained the captive audience with such feats as spinning around until she was dizzy, scrunching her nose and lips to make an obnoxious breathing sound through her nostrils, and making faces at the people behind us. I, of course, felt delighted to have such a cute and precocious child.

I had moved up to second in line when Kristen started to turn her attention toward me.

Her mother. The woman who had agonized fourteen hours, surviving on ice chips alone, to bring her into this world.

She began to focus her attention—all eighteen months' worth—on me. The woman who thought the sun rose and set on her, this precious child.

"Next," said the teller.

I stepped to the window and plopped the proceeds of a week-end garage sale on the marble countertop. The proceeds consisted of $717.83—mostly in quarters, nickels, and three pennies.

I glanced back to check on Kristen and then rested my elbows on the countertop, leaning forward and relaxing, just taking it easy and thinking how I was going to spend all that money.

This is the point where Kristen directed her attention fully to me.

I felt a small, tentative poke on my, err, backside.

I ignored it.

Bad decision.

Then another small—but decidedly stronger than the first—poke against my backside, accompanied by a singsong voice proclaiming, "Big bottom, Mom! Big bottom!"

Poke, poke. Prod, prod.

I whipped around and saw my three-foot munchkin grinning from ear to ear. Bolstered by the smiles and chuckles from those in her immediate vicinity, she kept poking and declaring. I lowered my head, unknotted my shirt, and whispered delicately, "Kristen, stop poking Mommy—and quit saying 'big bottom.'"

She appeared to understand what I was saying, so I continued, "It isn't nice to talk about Mommy's bottom. Now don't say 'bottom' again."

I turned back to Teller Girl, who was trying to quell a smirk, with dismal results.

Not a peep was heard from behind me.

Good.

Uh, scratch that. The silence following my little chat with Kristen was not good. She had used those brief moments for thinking, and now the small poke flourished into an all-out punch. With her tiny yet accurate pointer finger aiming for the rear, Kristen proclaimed for everyone, teller and glass-ensconced manager alike, to hear: "Big butt, Mommy, big butt!"[22]

Is it any wonder I have issues?

You quit telling thinner women, "I wish I were as skinny as you"? Without the discerning nature of grace we tend to make assumptions about other women's lives. This became glaringly apparent to me after a weekend conference during which I had commented about grace in action. In a rather off-the-cuff manner I quipped, "Ladies, let's quit telling women who are thinner than us that they are lucky. . . . Let's quit telling them that we wish we could eat anything we wanted and stay so thin."

One comment. But oh, the response it gleaned! Woman after woman approached me afterward and thanked me for saying those words.

"Julie," one woman told me through tears, "all my life I have fought to gain weight—any weight! All my life I have wished that I could look like a real woman—someone with curves, rather than angular planes. Ever since I was a girl in grade school, I have been disliked for being thin. But what those girls and women have never stopped to consider is that I disliked my being thin more than they did."

Grace stops—thinks—and assumes nothing.

You ate whenever you were hungry?
INCONCEIVABLE. Why, this scandalous consideration borders on heresy! Verily, verily, I say unto ye, the very foundations of the Diet Industry would collapse if such doctrine were adopted by women.

After eating whenever you were hungry, you felt NO GUILT?
I'm thinking 99.9 percent of panged female consciences relate somehow to food consumption. I could plaster this page with all sorts of statistical data about bulimia, anorexia, and other food-

related disorders. I could also list the FDA guidelines for healthy eating. But for many of us, it's nearly impossible to see food as anything but the enemy.

What if, instead, you are the one who declares, "Let's stop the war?" And you choose to lay down this weapon against yourself and others?

And we're not done yet. . . .

WHAT IF:

Your past didn't define who you are?

In a perfect world (one God promises will come) all things will become as new and the old will be completely done away with.[23] The harebrained ideas that you acted on as a fifteen-year-old will no longer haunt you. The choices you made—in fits of anger, passion, or rebellion—will no longer determine what you do and where you go.

In a world seized by grace, we'll throw off the misconceptions based on our parental lineage or ethnic background and be free to be who we were created to be. And in the meantime, we can demonstrate such truth to ourselves and those around us. We'll talk more about this in the next chapter.

You went a day without checking off a list of accomplishments?

Some of us keep track of things with a stylus and Palm Pilot. Others remain faithful to their tried-and-true, paper-and-pen Franklin Planner. One way or another, women everywhere are checking off things to do, places to go, people to see—and feeling mighty tired in the process.

Have you ever wanted to throw that stupid beeping pager

in the trash or "lose" your cell phone? Have you ever prayed for deliverance from the urge to check your E-mail every two minutes? *(Yes, I speak from experience!)*

Have you ever wondered what it would be like to wake up and simply allow the day to *happen* instead of hitting the ground running in your bare feet with a mental list of things to accomplish in the coming hours? Have you ever simply wanted to rest? And feel as though your day mattered—despite the fact that three or four things might remain unchecked?

You could live without guilt for not meeting someone else's expectations?

I came home the other evening and found thirteen messages on my answering machine and twenty-two in my E-mail box. *(I know, I know! But I swear I didn't check them every two minutes!)* Two of the E-mails and one of the phone messages were from angry listeners who vehemently disagreed with something I had said during a radio interview. The remaining twelve voice messages, as well as fifteen of the twenty other E-mails, were largely upbeat—complimentary and cheerful.

But which messages do you think stuck with me? Of course— the ones in which I had failed to meet the expectations of the listeners or E-mail writers.

I immediately corresponded with those that I could.

And for what purpose? Well, if I'm completely honest, it was to convince them that their impressions of me were wrong. I never really stopped and considered if their expectations of me were realistic or far-fetched. I simply did what so many of you have done—I felt bad for not meeting them.

You embraced your place in life?

No one laments *(not complaining, mind you, it's* lamenting*)* better than I do. Trust me, I know how to pour on the wailing and gnashing of teeth. I've run a gamut of lamentable matters by God and any breathing human willing to listen: communities we've lived in because of job transfers, rental properties, timing of pregnancies, financial messes, my inability to clap (in rhythm) and sing at the same time, as well as important matters regarding my children, parents, spouse, and me. It took me some time to realize that my lamenting was really getting me nowhere. I still had to live in the crummy communities. The rental properties I found still had to be cleaned and made into a home. My pregnancies—while not planned—had to be tended to and accepted. Eventually, grace brought me to a place not of hopeless resignation, but rather of joyous acceptance of the "right here, right now" realities of my living.

You quit buying magazines that showcase homes you can't afford and clothes you can't wear?

Okay, I'll admit, this scandalous thought borders on the meddlesome! But we'd all benefit from the thoughtful consideration of the graceless manner in which we regard our bodies, our homes, our possessions, and clothes. And how those thoughts are enmeshed in the marketing doctrine we consume through the pages of *My House Is Prettier than Yours* or *Lifestyles of 0.1 Percent of the Population.*

You prayed more than you thought about the size of your thighs?

This is going to be one of those confessions that will prove—if you're still not totally convinced—that I am a mess of magnificent proportions.

It was a Sunday morning, and I was standing next to my daughter and husband during the music portion of our service. Our church has an outstanding worship team and band, and I look forward to these moments the entire week. The atmosphere is one of relaxed worship, and people are free to lift their hands in praise or to keep them by their sides. There's no pressure one way or another—the service centers around the grace of each individual to worship.

So there I was, standing next to my daughter, listening to the lyrics of Michael W. Smith's song, "Above All," and sensing the intangible presence of God in our midst. I lifted my hands in worship: "Above all kingdoms, above all thrones. . . ." Opening my eyes, I gazed at those near me, caught up in the power of corporate, unified worship. And I too raised my voice and proclaimed, "Above all wonders the world has ever known. . . ."

That's when it happened. With arms raised, eyes now closed, and no one looking around, I realized a brain synapse had just occurred, and I found myself thinking, *Are my thighs touching? I know they weren't touching when I wore these pants a few weeks ago.*

A certifiable mess—wouldn't you agree?

You believed God was crazy about you?

Well, on the bright side, Michael W. Smith's song impacted the life of one of my favorite authors, Brennan Manning.

In his classic, *The Ragamuffin Gospel,* Brennan single-handedly introduced me to the initial concept of the outrageous grace and love of God . . . toward me. Conceptually I already knew about it. I had read the Bible, memorized verses, deconstructed Greek and Hebrew meanings, and immersed myself in inductive Bible studies. Theoretically I understood the love of God. But it wasn't until I recognized myself as a "bent, broken, and bedraggled" Christian, "whose cheese has fallen off [her] cracker," that I embraced—confessed—and believed that God was crazy about me. I had read Philip Yancey's modern-day parable of the prodigal child years before, but it was Brennan's gentle admonishment, "I could more easily contain Niagara Falls in a tea cup than I can comprehend the wild, uncontainable love of God,"[24] that transposed, for me, the love of the Father from concept to melodious creed.

Indeed, "it's in Christ that we find out who we are and what we are living for. Long before we first heard of Christ and got our hopes up, he had his eye on us, had designs on us for glorious living, part of the overall purpose he is working out in everything and everyone."[25]

Ladies, imagine how such thinking could change our lives. How it could change the way you live and act.

Instead of looking at one another and assuming.

Instead of living under a burden of rules and regulations.

Instead of denying the marvelous and fantastic love of God for you.

Why not revel in the *audacious* acts of divine grace and *boldly* exhibit the *dazzling* reality of such truth to others?

* 14 *

ℒET ℐT 𝒢O!

$\mathcal{I}$ am an appreciator of quips, one-liners, and zappy zingers. And if those zingers can express eternal truth—well, then, all the better.

As a young mother working to change her often sarcastic and hurtful tone toward her children, I began to say the following: *Julie, in the light of eternity, does this really matter?* It amazed me how many things fell under the category of "not really" when I applied that inquiry to the matter at hand.

In the light of eternity—does it really matter that my eight-year-old's hair is sticking up all over her head? Not really.

In the light of eternity—does it matter if her hair is sticking up all over her head before her first-grade Christmas program? Not really.

In the light of eternity—does it really matter that I can no longer fit into a single-digit jean size? Not really.

In the light of eternity . . .

That's a mighty big perspective to compare things to, wouldn't you agree? And here's the thing. When we ask ourselves, "In the light of eternity, does this matter?" we need to be prepared to answer this in response: "In the light of eternity—what does matter?"

Robert Frost wrote in his timeless poem of the *The Road Not Taken*:

Two roads diverged in a yellow wood,
And sorry I could not travel both
And be one traveller, long I stood
And looked down one as far as I could
To where it bent in the undergrowth;

Then took the other, as just as fair,
And having perhaps the better claim,
Because it was grassy and wanted wear;
Though as for that, the passing there
Had worn them really about the same,

And both that morning equally lay
In leaves no step had trodden black.
Oh, I kept the first for another day!
Yet knowing how way leads on to way,
I doubted if I should ever come back.

I shall be telling this with a sigh
Somewhere ages and ages hence:
Two roads diverged in a wood, and I—
I took the one less traveled by,
And that has made all the difference.[26]

Two roads diverged.

I took the one less traveled. . . .

And that has made all the difference.

In the light of eternity, I believe it is a single choice made during our time on earth that matters. Each of us walking the road called Life will be confronted with God's proverbial "fork in the road" personified in the life of Jesus Christ. And each will be compelled to individually answer this timeless question: Does Christ alone represent the "interlude of grace" between God and humanity?

I believe the answer is yes. Now, I could try to impress you with a bunch of theological terms to back up my supposition, but I don't believe that convinces many people of anything. I could overwhelm you with a bunch of Bible verses or list the top worst sins I think you could commit, but I'm not. I'm simply going to tell you what I have found to be true in my own journey of scandalous grace: We're all in need of a Divine Savior to forgive us from sin. Why? Because we're all a mess of magnificent proportions! Here's truth: Jesus Christ forgave my sins—sins that would make your toes curl if I confessed them to you. And this same Jesus has remained faithful despite forays in rebellion, depression, spiritual and near-financial bankruptcy, doubting, angry motherhood, and flat-out unbelief.[27] Jesus Christ is unlike anyone you have ever known—and when you choose to walk the road less traveled that leads to him, you will be given a fuller life for here—and all eternity.

Delicately knit and intertwined within the light of eternity are these three powerful words: *Let it go.* If you were to ask me for a definition of grace, I would respond, "Let it go." If you were to read the New Testament gospels—Matthew, Mark, Luke, and John—and consider the life of Jesus Christ and the way he interacted with women, I believe you would hear him say, time and time again, "Let it go."

Consider the woman caught in the act of adultery.

For those who have been raised in church and fed a steady diet of flannel-board stories as a child in Sunday school or church catechism, this may seem redundant. But stay with me, for there is a fresh perspective to take away from this oft-repeated account. And it is filled with the scandalous message of "let it go" grace that is available to any woman who will hear.

John writes, "The religion scholars and Pharisees led in a woman who had been caught in an act of adultery. They stood her in plain sight of everyone and said, . . ."[28]

Are you cringing? Or have you heard this story so many times that you don't even think about it anymore?

Four words in the middle of his opening statement bring it all home for me.

Caught.
In.
An.
Act.

Can you even imagine such humiliation? Being seen and caught participating in a sexual act?

My heart goes out to this woman from the very beginning. Not because I think what she has been caught doing is okay, but because I assume that as she was dragged away to be brought before Jesus, she was left in what she was wearing. Nothing. She was, in all likelihood, naked.

Can you begin to imagine the shame of standing naked before an audience? For that's just what John tells us happened: "They stood her in plain sight of everyone. . . ."

✳ ✳ ✳

I've read that the majority of Americans, when asked what they fear most, answer, "public speaking." I, on the other hand, think quite differently—"being seen naked!" I can think of nothing more shaming than this. About nine years ago, when my oldest child was about six years old and my second child was five, I actually prayed this prayer: "Dear God, please don't let me die naked." That morning I had slipped on a sliver of slimy soap and found myself on the tub floor looking up the faucet spout. And while the fall was painful, worse yet was the thought of my children—or, gads, the local volunteer rescue squad—finding me splayed out dead and undressed on the floor.

But it is here we find the woman—naked before Jesus and her accusers with nothing to cover herself.

The religious teachers then pointed out to Jesus that this woman had been caught red-handed. She had no excuse. She had no other story to tell. They had found her. She had been busted big-time. And so they continued, trying to trap Jesus into saying something—anything—against the Law, against religious "propriety," so they could charge him with heresy.

But Jesus didn't say a word to them. Nor does John tell us that he spoke to the adulteress. Instead, "Jesus bent down and wrote with his finger in the dirt."[29]

We have no idea what he wrote. Everything we may come up with is conjecture . . . speculation at best. But whatever it was, it wasn't anything that would silence her accusers. They continued to harp and badger Jesus to make a statement of some sort regarding what should be done—lawfully done—with a woman such as her.

Instead, Jesus straightened up and said, "'The sinless one among you, go first: Throw the stone.' Bending down again, he wrote some more in the dirt."[30]

No one badgered him this time. This time they walked away, one after another, beginning with the oldest. And within moments the woman was left alone.

I've often wondered if she had remained standing throughout this whole shameful interaction. If she did, then surely her eyes were squeezed shut, her head bowed, and she made eye contact with absolutely no one. Or perhaps she had fallen into a heap at Jesus' feet, curled up tightly into a fetal position, breathing dirt from the ground she had pressed her face against.

Then we read, "Jesus stood up and spoke to her, 'Woman, where are they? Does no one condemn you?'"

Looking up cautiously from the dirt or perhaps directly at Jesus for the first time, she responds, "No one, Master."

And she was right. No one was there to accuse her. No one was there to throw a stone, to kill her. There was simply Jesus.

"'Neither do I,' said Jesus. 'Go on your way. From now on, don't sin.'"[31]

✳ ✳ ✳

I consider all the things he, as the Son of God and teacher of the Law, could have said—rightfully said—to her. Words such as, "You tramp." "You're worthless." "You've earned what the Law says you get." If all I could know as a woman about this man Jesus was in this part of chapter 8 in the book of John, it would be enough. Every time I read this, I am swept away by the simplicity of his love and the magnitude of his grace.

I read aloud his words: "Go on your way. From now on, don't sin," and I hear the scandalous message of the divine. And Jesus' response convinces me all the more that he is like no other man. He truly *is* the divine, exemplifying divine, scandalous grace.

For years I've heard these Bible verses preached. I've heard the voices of men thunder from behind their pulpit, "And Jesus said, go and sin no more!!!!!!!!!!" But what my female heart hears . . . above the shouting and the somewhat harsh pastoral admonishment . . . is the gentlest of voices speaking three words of unfettering grace: "Let it go."

"Let it go," he says to her.

"Let it go," he says to you and me.

Let it go and stop doing the things that are killing you, stop doing the things that are suffocating your soul, stop doing the things that are poisoning your heart and separating you from me. Let it go, step back, take a look, gain a fresh perspective, and choose a road less traveled.

The culture in which you and I live is inundated with buzzwords and things we "have to do." But God doesn't want you to crazily "do" things for him; he wants to BE with you and to develop your heart like his. God wants *you*—more than anything. Once you've been graced by the scandal of the divine, your vision and perspective *always* change.

✳ ✳ ✳

And one of the best new perspectives we can embrace is this: Jesus doesn't care.

Do I have your attention? I thought so.

Now, wait a minute, you may be thinking. *What do you mean, Julie, that Jesus doesn't care?*

After all, I've spent a lot of time developing the concept that God loves you and me so much. That he cares so passionately about you and me that he broke all propriety and favored us, graced us, with his Son and with himself. So, after saying all those things in so many words, then I declare in a twilight chapter that Jesus doesn't care?

What's my point?

My point is this: Jesus knows where you've been and what sins you've committed there. Jesus knows what you've really thought. Jesus knows how many times you've broken a vow to "get it together." Jesus knows what you weigh, how many service awards you've won, or how many hours you've volunteered at the Red Cross.

Jesus knows all of these things—and yet he doesn't care about things. Jesus cares about YOU.

You. The woman whose presence he has known about since before time began. *(Incomprehensible.)*

You. The woman whose sins would make the stoutest priest blanch.

You. The woman—not the label of mom, career woman, divorcée, or the "other woman."

You. Jesus cares about you.

For it is within us that he begins to work. It is within us—in the depths of our creation—that he begins to weave a tapestry of grace. And it is to you—with your cartload of "issues" and journal full of "scorched places"—that he longs to say, "Neither do I condemn you. Go and sin no more."

At some point, in this process of surrendering to grace, we have to surrender to the Giver of all grace. Without that surrendering there can be no life transformation. We must surrender our very selves. Surrender our past. Surrender our present. And surrender to the promise of a glorious future.

Jesus Christ IS the Giver of grace! Grace and truth are realized in him alone.[32]

And this Grace Giver has used our scorched places to make us thirst for what we could never quench alone. This Grace Giver has placed one "lily pad" after another across our swamps of fear and doubting. And this Grace Giver is able to fill us to overflowing—able to reach the depth, the length, the width, and the height,[33] with the lavish richness of his intense chartreuse love, salvation through Christ, fellowship through the Holy Spirit, and communion with God the Father.

* 15 *

ℒIVING WITH ℒOOSE ℰNDS

FALL 1986

The first things I noticed were the color and shape of her hands and fingernails.

Olive complexion.

Small knuckles.

Thin nails.

Yes, they were familiar.

In the background chatter around me someone commented, "She sure doesn't look much like her, does she?" I brushed aside the words. I was compelled instead to look at the wheelchair in which she was sitting.

She being my birth mother. And this was the first time in my adult life that I had seen her. She's a double amputee, having lost both legs, just above the knee, in a motor vehicle accident while in her late twenties. "In her late twenties"—just a brief time after she had signed away parental rights for five of her *seven* children.

There are *six* living siblings at the time of the reunion, I learn, as a red-haired female steps forward and tells me she's my baby sister. She has freckles on her face. Are her hands freckled too? Well, I don't even look. I've already decided we look nothing alike.

As a twenty-one-year-old at the time of this first "reunion," I had been unwilling to face all this reality alone. So, gathering my trusted girlfriends (Lesa W. and Lisa C.) with me, we drove to the reunion. They promised to stay close by my side and "to get you out of there" if need be.

There was no need. I stayed for hours . . . touching my birth mother's hands, looking at Lynn's face, and finding the gaze of an older sister smiling back. I laughed with Beth and challenged both her and Lynn's memories of our time spent with "Aunt Bonnie."

"Beth, do you remember pushing Lynn off the bed in the blue bedroom and making her nose bleed?"

She didn't remember.

"Lynn, do you remember the swing set that sat next to the huge garden? Do you remember me getting my pinkie finger stuck in the chain and you freeing it?"

She didn't remember.

Then I dared to ask what I had wondered about for all those lonely years. "Do you remember getting in the car that day—*and leaving me?*"

The car and ice cream they remembered.

✷ ✷ ✷

On that day I met a paternal grandmother; an uncle named Melvin, who possessed a marvelous sense of humor; and three cousins from my birth father's side of the family. I was reunited with two older sisters and discovered a younger one. After years of praying and wondering, I came face-to-face with the woman who had given me life and saw for the first time whose hands I had. At last it appeared I would be able to tie up the loose ends of my life. Somehow I thought seeing my mother's hands would do just that. I thought sharing a childhood memory with my sisters would bring that. I thought confronting my past would magically, forever and always, heal my future.

But it didn't happen.

My birth mother and I were unable to establish a relationship. For three or four years we shared letters and a phone conversation or two, but too many questions (my questions) were left unanswered—or as I often felt, evaded. I was never able to comfortably "fit" her into the life I shared with Mom and Dad. I felt guilty for the cards she mailed my children and signed *Grandma G.* An afghan she had sent was stored in the box it arrived in, its "thinking of you" message too much to deal with. Facts and stories that I had overheard and been told as a child began to conflict with the information that she and both my sisters were giving.

Who should I believe?

Had someone lied to me?

Had anyone ever told me the truth?

Beth and I were unable to find common ground to join us as sisters, and Lynn somehow got stuck in the middle—playing mediator between a sister she had lived with her entire life and another she had never known. All the illusions and fantasies that I had created came tumbling down around my feet.

I had wanted my story to read: *Adopted Girl Resolves All Issues*. But the truth was (and still remains) that I may never have closure. Certainly not the earthly "wrap-up" that I was so hoping would occur:

✳ A birth mother who could emotionally make up for the lost years.

✳ Sister connections that remind me of the Johnson girls' relationship.

✳ That incredible feeling of absolute completeness.

Real life is anything but neat and tidy. It's about living with all the "loose ends."

✳ Loose ends dangling about the frayed edges of your heart and the scars of your soul.

✳ Loose ends exposing the seams of life.

✳ Loose ends that spill out and over the stuffed emotional constraints of simplistic religious thought.

I'm thirty-seven years old at the writing of this chapter and haven't spoken to my birth mother in nearly ten years. Trust me, this is one of the dangliest loose ends in my life. After all, it isn't like she's still out there—unknown, unnamed, unattainable. I know her name, where she lives. I could dial a number and hear her voice or jump in my car and drive to meet her. But I can't. I just haven't been able to find a way to make her—us—fit.

Despite my joy at seeing the hands that resembled mine, I haven't been able to embrace them. Often enough over the years, I've thought, *Maybe there's something wrong with me.* I've even talked about it with counselors. But the jury is still out.

Meanwhile, the loose ends remain.

Lynn and Beth and I share a distant, if not tenuous, relationship. The sisters I had fantasized about do not exist. They didn't even remember *me* from that day in 1968. And while the "think about this like an adult" side of me understands the magnitude of their loss and the reality that they have had to block things from memory just to get by, it still feels like a wound that's been reopened. A scab that's been picked. And it still hurts and sends me hurtling back to those few cherished memories with one another, piecing the loose ends together, stringing them along . . . hoping to convince myself that I hadn't made it all up.

I recall a famous nighttime soap opera that began its season opener with one of the main characters walking out of his shower and finding his (until that moment "dead") wife lying in their bed. It seems everything that he had lived the previous season hadn't actually happened. It had all been a dream— an ugly nightmare. In this fanciful, and in my humble opinion, moronic fashion, the producers attempted to wrap up the loose ends of the previous season.

But I've often felt as though I were living in such a melodramatic fashion.

Wondering if I had "made up" the feelings and the memories from early childhood.

Wondering if I had somehow invented the emotions of grief regarding the scorched places of life.

And wondering if I had, in fact, finally awoken, only to discover that my entire early childhood had been one big, bad, ugly dream, after all.

Loose ends can make you seriously question your sanity.

So let me say it again, life is not neat and tidy. I'm not sure it was ever meant to be. Well, I take that back. I believe there was such a time. In a garden, one filled with all a woman could ever want—and all a woman would need. But the mesmerizing allure for things just out of reach obscured her vision and caused her to walk down a road never meant to be traveled—ending in tragic consequences. There was another time and another place where loose ends never existed, but that place is no more.[34]

At least for the interim between earth and heaven.

This life—our life—is not about finding or getting closure on certain areas of life. It's about a God, a divine Father, who is there with us IN THE MIDST. (Jesus promised us such in John 14:18: "I will not leave you orphaned," as well as assuring us that he doesn't want us to feel abandoned, bereft, upset, or distraught.)[35] It is about living a life that recognizes it is only as we open up to one another about our struggles and only as we begin extending exquisite grace to each other in the scorched places that we stand a prayer of experiencing healing. True divine healing.

It is Eugene H. Peterson, noted pastor, scholar, writer, poet, and author of *The Message: The Bible in Contemporary Language,* that I quoted in the chapter titled "Scorched Places." With the subtitle *A Full Life in the Emptiest of Places,* Peterson wove a tapestry of words and phrases, depicting with startling clarity God's desire toward us: "I will always show you where to go. I'll give you a full life in the emptiest of places."[36]

And for those yearning for such refreshment but still wondering what good can come from their pain, their emptiness, their loose ends that pepper the landscape of past and present, he reminds us yet again, "You'll use the old rubble of past lives to build anew, rebuild the foundations from out of your past. You'll be known as those who can fix anything, restore old ruins, rebuild and renovate, make the community livable again."[37]

What crazy architect would allow his work to be built with broken, fragmented pieces of material?

I smile and shout, "God!"

God loves to work with rubble. He relishes the opportunity to take things considered worthless and redeem them to something of incomprehensible value.

God rollicks in doing the seemingly impossible and in flaunting the "this will never work" or "you can never be used" propriety of man.

God delights in restoring women to grace and faith—and joy and laughter.

God wallows in rebuilding lives to his glory.

And God kicks up his heels at the task of renovating—down to the smallest detail—every room of our body, heart, mind, and soul.

So what remains? Simply this: hearken back to the story of my grandmother's outrageously iced angel food cake. Remember the lavish doling of the cream-cheese frosting? Lavish enough that I could run my finger along its side and go four inches before I hit cake? Lavish enough that puddles of plentiful icing pooled along the serving platter?

Take that imagery now, girls, and place YOURSELF on the platter. Place yourself on the platter of life and just dare the Divine Father to coat you with a serving of scandalous, outrageous, preposterous, divine grace!

GRACE PERSPECTIVES

These quotes have acted as stepping-stones on my own journey toward understanding scandalous grace. Perhaps they'll do the same for you.

Grace is uncontrollable, arbitrary to our senses, apparently unmerited. It's utterly free, ferociously strong, about as mysterious a thing as you could imagine. First rule of grace: grace rules.

> —Brian Doyle, quoted in *The Best Spiritual Writing 2001,* edited by Philip Zaleski[38]

Grace overcomes shame, not by uncovering an overlooked cache of excellence in ourselves but simply by accepting us, the whole of us, with no regard to our beauty or our ugliness, our virtue or our vices. We are accepted wholesale. Accepted with no possibility of being rejected. Accepted once and accepted forever. Accepted at the ultimate depth of our being.

> —Lewis B. Smedes in *Shame and Grace*

Now I'm turning you over to God, our marvelous God whose gracious Word can make you into what he wants you to be and give you everything you could possibly need in this community of holy friends.
—Acts 20:32

Grace can never be possessed but can only be received afresh again and again.
—Rudolf Bultmann

God gives his gifts where he finds the vessel empty enough to receive them.
—C. S. Lewis, quoted in *God Hunger* by John Kirvan

In becoming grace, you start from a place of emptiness. When you empty of expectations, you open to the wonders that happen in moments and nanoseconds of revelation. With God's grace active in you, nothing can go wrong. Every thought, word, and action, when joined with grace, will be formless and serve goodness.
—Shoni Labowitz in *Miraculous Living*

For all have sinned and fall short of the glory of God, being justified as a gift by His grace through the redemption which is in Christ Jesus.
—Romans 3:23-24, NASB

You are seeking for secret ways of belonging to God, but there is only one: making use of whatever God offers you.
—Jean-Pierre de Caussade, quoted in *Praying Dangerously* by Regina Sara Ryan

We think of grace arriving like an ambulance, just-in-time delivery, an invisible divine cavalry cresting a hill of troubles, a bolt of jazz from the glittering horn of the Creator, but maybe it lives in us and is activated by illness of the spirit. Maybe we're loaded with grace. Maybe we're stuffed with the stuff. Maybe it's stitched into our DNA, a fifth ingredient in the deoxyribonucleic acidic soup.

    —Brian Doyle, quoted in *The Best Spiritual Writing 2001*, edited by Philip Zaleski[39]

Grace, because God is putting everything together again through the Messiah, invites us into life—a life that goes on and on and on, world without end.

    —Romans 5:21

Our own experiences of grace give an inchoate meaning to the stories of our lives. They hint at purposes which exist beyond ourselves.

    —Andrew M. Greeley in *God in Popular Culture*

Grace teaches truth, . . . illumines the soul, produces tears.

    —Thomas à Kempis, quoted in *The Imitation of Christ*, edited by William Griffin

For you know the grace of our Lord Jesus Christ, that though He was rich, yet for your sake He became poor, that you through His poverty might become rich.

    —2 Corinthians 8:9, NASB

Grace is the light or electricity or juice or breeze that takes you from that isolated place and puts you with others who are as startled and embarrassed and eventually grateful as you are to be there.

—Anne Lamott in *Traveling Mercies*

But to each one of us grace was given according to the measure of Christ's gift.

—Ephesians 4:7, NASB

Grace happens to me when I feel a surge of honest joy that makes me glad to be alive in spite of valid reasons for feeling terrible. Grace happens when I accept my wife's offer to begin again with me in love after I have hurt her. It happens when I feel powerfully free to follow my own conscience in spite of those who think I am either crazy or wicked. Grace is the gift of feeling sure that our future, even our dying, is going to turn out more splendidly than we dare imagine. Grace is the feeling of hope.

—Lewis B. Smedes in *How Can It Be All Right When Everything Is All Wrong?*

But He gives a greater grace. Therefore it says, "God is opposed to the proud, but gives grace to the humble."

—James 4:6, NASB

When we open our hearts to each other we allow grace to enter. It is as simple as that. And suffering—events that break open the heart—can become the refiner's fire that leaves us fully open to the truth about love and compassion.

—Kathleen A. Brehony in *Ordinary Grace*

Grace to you and peace from God our Father, and the Lord Jesus Christ, who gave Himself for our sins, that He might deliver us out of this present evil age, according to the will of our God and Father, to whom be the glory forevermore.

—Galatians 1:3-5, NASB

GRANDMA BONNIE'S TO-DIE-FOR ANGEL FOOD CAKE

1 cup of cake flour (Grandma preferred *Swan's Down* brand)
1½ cups white sugar
13 egg whites
1½ teaspoons vanilla extract
1½ teaspoons cream of tartar
½ teaspoon salt

Preheat the oven to 375 degrees. Be sure your 10″ tube pan is clean and dry. Any amount of oil or residue could deflate the egg whites. Sift together the flour and one cup of the sugar; set aside.

In a large bowl, whip the egg whites along with the vanilla, cream of tartar, and salt, until they form medium-stiff peaks. Gradually add the remaining sugar (2 tablespoons at a time) while continuing to whip to stiff peaks. When the egg mixture has reached its maximum volume, fold in the sifted ingredients gradually, one third at a time. Do not overmix. Pour the batter into ungreased tube pan. Gently cut through batter with metal spatula to ensure uniformity of batter.

Bake for 40–45 minutes in the preheated oven until the cake springs back when touched. Balance the tube pan upside down on its legs to prevent decompression while cooling. If your pan does not have these "legs," simply balance it over a couple of cans. When cool, run a knife around the edge of the pan and invert onto a plate or platter.

ICING:
2 - 8-ounce packages cream cheese, softened (do not substitute with low-fat cheese)
½ cup butter, softened (do not substitute with margarine)
¼ cup half-and-half
2 teaspoons vanilla
5½ cups powdered sugar
1 tablespoon lemon juice (optional)

Beat cream cheese and butter until light and fluffy. Beat in vanilla. Gradually add powdered sugar. Add half-and-half to desired texture and add lemon juice if desired. Lavish cake when it is completely cooled. Enjoy!

ABOUT THE AUTHOR

Call her a twenty-first-century Erma Bombeck with a pleas-antly skewed twist! Julie Ann Barnhill's outrageous humor will indeed have you "laughing so hard you snort" and clap-ping your hands with glee. With her disarming wit and gener-ous doses of vulnerability and authenticity, both on stage and in print, she's become a best-selling author and popular national speaker.

Julie's first featured book, *She's Gonna Blow! Real Help for Moms Dealing with Anger,* caught the attention of American television and radio producers nationwide, as did her most recent publication, *'Til Debt Do Us Part: Real Help for Couples Dealing With Finances,* in Canada and Britain. Julie has appeared on such programs as: *Oprah, CNN Sunday Morning,* Dick Clark's *The Other Half,* CNBC's *PowerLunch,* and the Canadian televi-sion show *It's a New Day.* Her radio spots include: *National Public Radio, Janet Parshall's America,* the *Midday Connection* in Chicago, and a two-day interview that aired March 17–18, 2003, with radio legend Dr. James Dobson on *Focus on the Family Broadcasting.*

Julie is a spunky, sassy, and thought-provoking speaker. She challenges her audiences to "fasten their seat belts!" as she dispenses the lone antidote for remaining sane amidst life's roller-coaster ride of emotional, financial, physical, and spiritual ups and downs—the medicinal cure of guffaw-inducing, jaw-aching, "my stomach muscles hurt so much" laughter!

She is also the mother of three sometimes annoying, always amusing, challenging, stubborn, funny, and argumentative children. And wife to one hubby who has co-owned her dream of speaking and writing since 1984, the year they met. Amazingly, this man thinks she can do anything. (Okay, anything but mend clothes. Her motto is: If you lose a button, buy a new shirt. Got a hole in your sock? Go buy a twelve-pack.)

Julie, her husband, and their three dependents live in a small (population 486, including decorative yard dwarfs) village located in western Illinois. In that town people use riding lawn mowers as all-terrain vehicles. In fact, Julie about jumped out of her new-neighbor skin when John Deere and Snapper tractors sputtered to the post-office door! It's a place where entertainment is somewhat limited to pulling up a lawn chair and watching a neighbor trim his twenty-five-foot elm tree with a handsaw and rickety ladder. But it's also the kind of old-fashioned place where your neighbor makes you home-made meatballs in the middle of winter and brings them over "just because."

Rounding out her family is Tweety, the parakeet, who, at age four, has managed to outlive six cats and two dogs *(may they rest in peace).*

You can visit Julie Barnhill's Web site at: *www.juliebarnhill.com.*

If you are interested in having Julie Ann Barnhill speak at your special event, please contact her directly at her Web site or at *Julie@juliebarnhill.com*

ENDNOTES

[1] Frederick Buechner, *Now and Then* (San Francisco: HarperSanFrancisco, 1991).

[2] Ephesians 1:7-8, Eugene H. Peterson, *The Message* (Colorado Springs: NavPress, 2002), 2126.

[3] 2 Corinthians 12:9, ibid., 2110.

[4] Colossians 2:7, ibid., 2146.

[5] Romans 5:20, ibid., 2040–2041.

[6] Philip Yancey, *What's So Amazing About Grace?* (Grand Rapids, Mich.: Zondervan, 1997), 49-51. Used by permission.

[7] 2 Corinthians 9:9, Peterson, *The Message,* 2106.

[8] Romans 6:14, ibid., 2041.

[9] 2 Timothy 2:1, *New American Standard Bible* (LaHabra, Calif.: The Lockman Foundation, 1977), 1160.

[10] Beth Moore, *Breaking Free: Making Liberty in Christ a Reality in Life* (Nashville, Tenn.: Lifeway Church Resources, 1999).

[11] Julie Ann Barnhill, *'Til Debt Do Us Part* (Eugene, Oreg.: Harvest House Publishers, 2002), 109-112.

[12] Psalm 139:13-16, Peterson, *The Message,* 1081.

[13] Ephesians 1:4-5, ibid., 2126.

[14] Isaiah 58:11, ibid., 1323.

[15] Isaiah 58:12, ibid., 1324.

[16] Shea Gregory, "Confessions of a Sex Starved Single: What Should I Do with Raging Hormones?" *Today's Christian Woman,* (January/February 2000). As cited on-line at: http://www.christianitytoday.com/tcw/2000/001/4.46.html.

[17] Ephesians 2:2-5, Peterson, *The Message,* 2127.

[18] Romans 7:15, ibid., 2043.

[19] 2 Timothy 2:13, ibid., 2170.

[20] Anne Lamott, *Traveling Mercies* (New York: Pantheon Books, 1999), 3.

[21] Colossians 3:13-14, Peterson, *The Message,* 2148.

[22] Julie Ann Barnhill, *She's Gonna Blow! Real Help for Moms Dealing with Anger* (Eugene, Oreg.: Harvest House Publishers, 2001), 17–20.

[23] See 2 Corinthians 5:17.

[24] Brennan Manning, *The Ragamuffin Gospel* (Sisters, Oreg.: Multnomah Publishers, 2000), 162

[25] Ephesians 1:13, Peterson, *The Message,* 2126.

[26] As cited on-line at: http://www.amandashome.com/road.html, 18 March 2001.

[27] 2 Timothy 2:13, *The Message,* 2170.

[28] John 8:3, ibid., 1934.

[29] John 8:6, ibid., 1934.

[30] John 8:7-8, ibid., 1934.

[31] John 8:9-11, ibid., 1934.

[32] John 1:16-17, *New American Standard Bible* (LaHabra, Calif.: The Lockman Foundation, 1977), 1012.

[33] See Ephesians 3:18.

[34] Genesis 2:8—3:24, Peterson, *The Message,* 23-26.

[35] John 14:18; 27, ibid., 1950-51.

[36] Isaiah 58:11, ibid., 1323.

[37] Isaiah 58:12, *The Message,* 1324.

[38] Brian Doyle, in *The Best Spiritual Writing 2001*, edited by Philip Zaleski (New York, NY: HarperCollins Publishers, 2001), 49.

[39] Ibid., 57-58.